Finding The Brand In You
Journey of an Introvert Becoming an Influencer

Orangebooks Publication

1st Floor, Rajhans Arcade, Mall Road, Kohka, Bhilai, Chhattisgarh 490020

Website: **www.orangebooks.in**

© **Copyright, 2024, Author**

All rights reserved. No part of this book may be reproduced, stored in a retrieval system, or transmitted, in any form by any means, electronic, mechanical, magnetic, optical, chemical, manual, photocopying, recording or otherwise, without the prior written consent of its writer.

First Edition, 2024
ISBN: 978-93-6554-351-3

FINDING THE
BRAND
IN
YOU

A Journey of an Introvert Becoming an Influencer

MANISH UPADHYAY

OrangeBooks Publication
www.orangebooks.in

Dedication

To all the hungry souls who believe in themselves and constantly strive for more.

To the parents who instil the belief in their children that they can pursue their passions and stand tall.

For everyone seeking to live life on their own terms, crafting their destiny rather than settling for the default.

Foreword

Empowerment through education is a foundational belief that aligns profoundly with the essence of Manish Upadhyay's book " Finding The Brand In You." I am happy to write this foreword, reflecting on the transformative journey and shared mission of empowering young minds that have brought Manish and his work to the forefront.

My initial encounter with Manish and his company, OPEN BOX Consulting, was in early 2016. Manish approached us with a proposal to conduct a skill-development training program as part of his corporate social responsibility initiative. Offered at a discounted price, the program was an instant success, leading to a partnership that has since seen over 58 programs conducted, training more than 3,600 girls. This collaboration has become an integral part of our Skill Development efforts, contributing to the knowledge and skills imparted to our beneficiaries.

At OPEN BOX Consulting, Manish and his team have been pivotal in advancing our Skill Development Program. Their expertise and commitment have enriched the lives of many young women, preparing them for the challenges of the professional world. The 'Self Reliance and Personal Development' workshop, which forms the basis of " Finding The Brand In You," stands out as one of the most successful programs. Conducted personally by Manish, whether online or offline, in cities like Amravati, Wardha, Nagpur, and recently in Hyderabad and Bengaluru, this workshop has been a transformative experience for our students. Manish has conducted this workshop over 45 times with our foundation, each time leaving a lasting impact on the participants.

His insights on the concept of 'Finding The Brand In You' have deeply resonated with our students, inspiring them to discover and cultivate their unique strengths and potential.

"Finding The Brand In You" is more than just a book; it is a movement encouraging individuals to recognise their inherent worth and capabilities. Manish's approach is practical, insightful, and deeply motivational, offering readers a roadmap to personal and professional growth.

As you read this book, you will embark on a journey of self-discovery. Manish's words serve as a guide, urging you to look within and unearth the 'brand' that is uniquely yours.

In closing, I express my heartfelt gratitude to Manish Upadhyay for his unwavering commitment to education and empowerment. His work has been a beacon of hope for many young students, lighting the path to a brighter future. "Finding The Brand In You" encapsulates this spirit of empowerment, and I am confident it will inspire countless readers to unlock their true potential. Manish, your dedication is truly inspiring.

With best wishes.

Mrs. Lila Poonawalla
(Recipient of The Padma Shri Award, 1989)
Chairperson,
Lila Poonawalla Foundation

Acknowledgement

I want to express my heartfelt gratitude to all my mentors who have played a pivotal role in shaping me into the person I am today.

Firstly, my father, Manoj, who has been my constant companion in sharing my dreams. His patient listening and guidance have instilled in me the determination and attitude that I possess. He is my ultimate inspiration.

My mother, Pushpa, shares a special bond with me, especially since the onset of COVID-19 when I started working from home. We've grown closer; now, even a moment apart feels incomplete. She epitomises care in every sense.

To my elder brother, Prashant, whose thought-provoking questions have always sparked new ideas within me. He constantly uplifts and motivates me to strive for more.

My wife, Shilpa, deserves special mention for enduring my passion and hectic schedule with unwavering patience. Despite my constant chatter about my book, she has been my pillar of support and the backbone of our family.

My sister-in-law, Khushboo, for her continuous indirect support and caring nature.

To my son Sheel and nephew Neil, although I couldn't always play with them due to my commitments, I hope they'll be proud of me when they read this book. They are both dreamers in their own right, with Neil being an avid reader.

My best friend, Milind, has an unparalleled understanding and trust in me. His invaluable advice and unwavering support have enabled me to unlock my true potential. I feel truly blessed to have him as a friend.

My friend and scooter companion, Nilesh, who shares my business vision and values. He understands my background, including my roots and challenges.

I am immensely grateful to my consulting teammates, Visshesh Prasad, Rutika Meshkar, Rizwiya, Rishi, and Ankit, who stepped up and handled a significant portion of my workload, allowing me to focus on my book.

A big shoutout to Ayushi for her genuine guidance throughout my writing journey. And my editor, Ritu Khurana, you really dove into my mindset (trust me, it's not easy), and you did a fantastic job. Thank you, Ritu, for your attentive listening, editing, and thought-provoking questions, as well as for putting your heart and soul into this book. Your support helped me reevaluate my writing approach—a huge thanks to you and the entire team at Rolling Authors.

I'd like to thank the **Lila Poonawala Foundation** and **The Indian Stammering Association** for inspiring me to embark on this writing journey. The idea first struck me during the numerous workshops I conducted on 'Brand in You' at the Lila Poonawala Foundation.

Finally, I extend my gratitude to my clients and students who have motivated me to expand my horizons and think beyond my limitations.

Prologue

2018

As I entered the darkened room, I realised I was at the back of the stage where I would speak in public for the first time! My heart raced as an announcement about the first speaker was going on stage, which would be me.

The MC told the crowd, "Can you imagine how you'd feel listening to someone who used to have trouble speaking and is now leading training programs? This stutterer is now up on the TEDx stage, sharing their story. It's pretty amazing, right?"

Crew members at the backstage smiled at me. I was so excited to tell the world how I became a speaker and trainer and what I learned through stuttering.

I cleared my throat, silently prayed to God, and entered the stage.

I liked talking the most, valuable speaking, as I could not speak properly in childhood. Having the stammer in my speech turned me into an introvert. I used to dream that someday I would share my life learning through a global platform, and today, this dream came true as God gave me this opportunity.

In 13 straight minutes, I became a TEDx speaker.

How did this happen? How did you overcome your stammering? How did you feel when people insulted you for being unable to speak properly? I get such questions all the time.

During my early days, I had faith in myself. I knew I was the only one who could help me and uplift me. It all started with me. It is more about personal development.

I meet many professionals and participants from various organisations, and I feel that the only thing that can help them is themselves. Many people focus on the "problem" but forget that the most significant resource of solution providers is themselves.

Everything you want in life may be success, wealth, and prosperity. It starts with you and is on the other side of your fear. It doesn't matter whether you are a corporate professional or businessman, Working woman or sales executive, consultant or self-employed professional. Everything starts with you.

So, if you want to achieve any victory, first achieve personal victory. Only then is it possible to achieve "Public Victory?"

I have mentioned some strategies for personal achievement in this book. Personal victory is always first, then comes public triumph.

I believe "The individual who cannot manage himself cannot manage the organisation."

To start working on personal triumph, the first thing you have to do is to create self-awareness.

Where do you want to reach? – This question helps you to understand where you are now!

Content

1. 2005 1
2. The Phone Call 6
3. Train to Nagpur 12

Day – 1
4. 6:00 AM | Attitude of Gratitude 18
5. 10:30 AM | No Excuse 23
6. 2:00 PM | The Start 30
7. 5:00 PM | Leadership: Seed of Every Action 41

Day – 2
8. 6:10 AM | Morning Rituals 56
9. 8:30 AM | Action Cures Fear 65
10. 11:15 AM | Communication 75
11. 2:30 PM | Attitude (You See What You Are) 92
12. 4:00 PM | Time Management 96

Day – 3
13. 5:45 AM | Belief 106
14. 8:15 AM | Habit Formation and Procrastination 112
15. 1:30 | Personality Development 117
16. 4 PM | Secrets of Champions 123
17. 7.00 PM | Brand in You 130
18. Life Lessons 138

Epilogue 141
19. 2018 141
20. About the Author 145

1

"Once you decide that you want better for yourself, the entire Universe begins to shift in your favour."

~ Anonymous

2005

It was a warm and pleasant afternoon in my hometown as my college results were declared. I was now a graduate and, finally, a mechanical engineer. I was eager to step out in the world, find a job, and start earning! But how? Who would hire me? More importantly, *why* would they hire me? I wasn't a topper, just an average student; nothing more, nothing less.

I had had a difficult childhood with my stammering problem. I was always the butt of jokes with my peers. It was a Catch-22 situation – the more they laughed at me, the less confident I became, and the more I stammered. As I grew up, the stammering lessened, but occasionally, I still stammered, especially when I was nervous.

I belonged to a business family. My father, Hiren *bhai* Patel, was in the restaurant business. I grew up seeing him work odd hours: waking up at 5 AM to prepare for the breakfast service, coming back home late at night after the dinner shift, and cleaning and closing the restaurant.

On the other hand, I was interested in a corporate job—more like a 9-5 thing—so I could give time to my family. On weekends and holidays, I worked with my father in the restaurant, doing odd jobs. Papa told me it was so that I could learn how the service industry works, talk to different kinds of people and learn to be humble. This immensely helped me become a little more confident. Unlike my peers, the older people were kind and encouraged me to talk.

I always took people at face value… I listened to how they talked and asked people for advice, especially on career matters. I had big dreams, but like most kids my age, I had no idea how to achieve them.

Oh, by the way, I am Mehul Patel. I am 22 years old and a Mechanical Engineer from Maharaja Sayajirao University (MSU, Baroda) in Vadodara, Gujarat, and this is my story.

There is no place like home to begin your journey. I started by asking my father for guidance.

"Papa, now that I've graduated, how and where should I start looking for a job? I… I… I…" I was nervous.

How do I tell my father I didn't want to work with him in the restaurant?

I would learn this much later in life, to be precise, when I became a dad myself, that a father knows, without spoken words, what his son wants.

"Mehul, *beta*," he said. "You don't have to worry about my restaurant. You do what you have to do, what you want to do, and apply for jobs in the field of your study. I don't know much about this area, but you can always call Amit *Bhai* for help. I'm sure he will be able to guide you well."

"Yes, Papa. Thank you," I said, hugging my father.

Amit Mehta, my father's closest friend, was a social guy and a people person. He ran a cyber cafe and met all kinds of people. He also ran a non-profit organisation that taught young minds and trained them in practical work skills. Through his work, he got connected with many people across boundaries. Although not well-educated, Amit *bhai* was always ready to lend a helping hand.

My father and his friends belonged to middle-class families who wanted to achieve something greater in life, if not for their own sake, then for the betterment of their children's futures.

I applied for many jobs in the next few days through newspaper ads and websites like Naukri.com. I was called for an interview at a few places, but I always got nervous and faced rejection because I couldn't answer properly, even though I knew my subject.

After the rejections, I felt miserable, but then I remembered that my father had told me to call Amit uncle for help. I was hesitant initially, but then I gathered my courage to call him. Amit uncle had this unique quality of making things happen through his connections.

"Hello, Amit uncle, how are you?" I finally called him.

"I'm good, Mehul *beta*. How are you? How's Hiren *bhai*? I hear you're an engineer now?"

"Yes, uncle. I'm now a mechanical engineer. And that's why I'm calling to ask for your help."

"Congratulations on your graduation, Mehul. Tell me, how can I help you?" asked Amit.

"Uncle, I want to achieve a great deal in my life and work with all my energy and power, but I'm unsure where to begin. I have applied for jobs in many companies but have not received proper responses, and where I have received responses, I.. I.. failed in the interviews."

"Hmmm…" said Amit thoughtfully. "Let me see what I can do about it."

Amit uncle called me back in a couple of hours.

"You know what, Mehul?" Amit uncle sounded excited. "There's this guy I know, Milind Fadnavis. He's based in Nagpur but came here a couple of years ago for a workshop at my NGO. I also brought him to your dad's restaurant a few times. Do you remember him?"

"Umm... no, uncle. I don't think I met him," I replied, trying to recall if I had ever met this guy.

"Oh, you may have missed meeting him because I used to bring him for lunch to your father's restaurant those few days he was here. You must be in college, then. Ask Hiren *bhai*. He should remember him," continued Amit uncle. "Anyway, Milind is a peak performance expert. He is a consultant with various organisations and trains senior professionals and business owners to perform better. He runs workshops and boot camps for determined young kids like you in his free time. His passion brought him to my NGO as well. I'm sure he will be able to guide you in the right direction. Let me talk to him about you today. I'll give you his number, and you can contact him tomorrow morning."

"Oh, sure, uncle. Please give me his number," I requested.

Amit uncle dictated the number to me, which I wrote down in my diary. I will call him tomorrow, but what should I say to him? How do I ask for help from someone I don't even know? These were the last thoughts running through my mind before sleep engulfed me.

2

"When We strive to become better than we are, everything around us becomes better, too."

~ **Anonymous**

The Phone Call

I built up my confidence the following morning and called Mr Fadnavis.

"Hello, Am I.. I speaking to Mr. Milind Fadnavis?" I enquired.

"Yes, who is this?" a deep voice came from the other end.

"This is Mehul Patel from Va.. Va.. Vadodara. Amit Uncle… Ugh, I mean, Mr Amit Mehta gave me your number and asked me to contact you. I.. I.. I want guidance for my career. Is thi- this the right time to talk?"

"*Haan*… Yes, I got a call from Amit *Bhai* yesterday about you. You are Hiren bhai's son, aren't you? How's he doing? I still remember the delicious food and the wonderful discussions we had during our lunch breaks," Milind said.

"Ye.. Yes, sir, I am. He's doing well, th.. thank you," I replied.

"Tell me, Mehul, how can I help you?" Milind asked. Even if he noticed my stammer, he didn't say anything. This gave me a little confidence.

"S- Sir, I just graduated from MSU in Baroda with a degree in Mechanical Engineering."

"Good for you, Mehul. Congratulations," he said coolly.

"I am an average student from a small city who wants a good job," I blurted.

"So, what's the problem?" asked Milind.

"N- No, no problem at all," I replied hurriedly. "I am searching for a job as a Maintenance Engineer, and I hope I will get one sooner or later, but I want to do more in life. I want something extra from life!"

"What do you mean by extra? Do you require guidance for a job, a career, or life? You decide first!" Milind said nonchalantly.

"Sir, of course, for a job, but... how do I explain this? I- I'm not getting the right words! You see, Mr Fadnavis, I will start working, like my seniors in many organisations, but I don't see the spark on their faces anymore, the spark that used to be there when they first joined their respective companies. I want to do something and not lose that spark from my face. Yes, I want to work for a company, but I just don't want to work for the sake of earning money. I want to grow as a professional and as a person and to keep learning in whatever life throws at me. I want more from a job, more from life, but I'm not sure how to get it," I said it all in one breath. "I.. I.. I hope I'm making sense to you."

"Hmm... Look, Mehul, I get where you're coming from. I see a lot of kids wanting more – but not willing to do anything about it. If you're on the hunt for a job or need a reference, I might not be your go-to guy. But, if you're keen on taking some ACTION STEPS to push forward in life, whatever path you're on, I'm here to lend a hand," Milind replied.

I listened, dumbfounded.

"Let me break it down for you," Milind continued. "Learning life strategies to push yourself forward covers way more ground than just landing a job. Think of it like a puzzle – a job is just one tiny piece. What are the other pieces? Figuring out how to start, why you're starting anything in the first place, and how to get what you truly want. If you're facing these questions, then I'm your guy. But if not, no worries, find someone who fits the bill better."

I'd never heard anything like this before. Although Papa motivated me to do more, nobody ever asked me questions about what **I wanted** and how I would get it. **ACTION STEPS.** This was all new for me, and this is when I decided to meet this guy, Milind Fadnavis. I was still deep in my thoughts when I heard the voice from the other end.

"Mehul, are you there? What are you thinking?" he asked.

I realised I had been silent for longer than required. "Sorry, sir. I- I just got lost thinking about what you said. I would like to meet you and learn about life and how to make things happen," Mehul replied cheerily.

"Hmm... okay. Let me think about it. How would you meet me? I'm in Nagpur, Maharashtra, and you're in Baroda, Gujarat. We're in 2 different states," Milind replied.

"No problem, sir. I will come to meet you in Nagpur," I was eager to meet this guy, as he had piqued my curiosity.

"But I have certain conditions," Milind said.

Conditions! Does he give assignments or homework? *Yaar*, I don't want this now! I'm done with homework! Or is he asking about something else? Or am I just overthinking now!!!

"Yes, sir? Umm... Wh.. What conditions?"

"If you come to Nagpur, I want you to stay here for three days. I will take care of everything, like your stay and food arrangements. But you have to be with me for three full days. You can ask your parents and then only decide. There's no compulsion," Milind said firmly.

"Umm... I guess I am okay with it," I replied, eager to accept all conditions.

"I don't want 'okay' people, Mehul." Milind continued, "I want people ready for themselves and ready to move to the next level. Your father may just be a decision-maker, but you are the only one who will change your life. So, take your time and decide. There's no hurry from my side. But if you say yes, then remember the three-day rule."

"Okay, sir... Oh, not okay. Yes, sir, I am sure I am coming," I blurted.

"Don't make such a quick decision. Ask your father first, discuss it with your family, and then decide. Is there anything else you want to ask me?" Milind asked.

Oh, hell yes! I had so many questions, but they can all wait. For now, I have to worry about asking Mr Fadnavis about the payment. I have to pay for my stay, food, and everything. Would this man charge something? Shall I ask him? All these thoughts were bubbling in my mind.

"Sure, sir. Could you tell me how much I would need to pay for lodging and boarding?"

"*Haan... Haan.* You young folks always focus on the here and now, right? I was like that when I was your age; I also used to think short-term always. But you know what? You've got some good questions there. Let me make things clear. I'll handle your accommodation and meals. You'll be staying with me at my home. Let me know if you're good with that for three days. And as for my fees, we'll talk about that later. Take some time to think it over and let me know your decision," Milind said.

I was now confident that this guy was very peculiar. What would he charge at the end? What would he ask? "Okay, Sir. I will ask my family and let you know by tomorrow evening."

"*Chalega.* Take your time."

"Thank you, sir, for giving your valuable time. It was nice to talk to you."

"My pleasure. Thank you. Take care, and all the best, Mehul."

"Thank You." I disconnected the call.

So, there I was, plopped down on a chair, letting my thoughts wander. You know that feeling when you realise nobody's ever been as direct, hopeful, and downright optimistic about your life except you? I've talked to plenty of people, but this was different. It's like this seven-minute chat just shook something deep inside, you know? It really got me thinking.

That evening, I went to the restaurant to talk to my father and try to convince him to let me go and stay with a stranger for three days. I had rehearsed the answers to all the different questions Papa might ask, and I was ready for the battle.

But my father, being my father, stumped me on the first ball! I didn't need to fight any battles. He had spoken with Amit uncle and was already convinced. I was worrying for nothing.

"Are you ready to take the plunge, Mehul?" Papa asked. "Don't miss this chance to meet him. I remember Milind as being a very knowledgeable guy. We used to discuss a lot of subjects over the lunches he had here. I'm sure he'll help you as best he can. It's a win-win situation. Not only will you get a break from the daily grind, but you'll also experience a change of scenery! And even if nothing else pans out, just think about all the lessons you'll learn from your first solo travel!"

Mehul decided to change his life and meet Milind Fadnavis in Nagpur.

3

*"Only I can change my life.
No one can do it for me."*

~ Carol Burnett

Train to Nagpur

A few days later, excitement bubbled within me as I boarded the train from Baroda to Nagpur. The journey felt like a bridge to a new beginning, with each passing mile bringing me closer to stepping into a fresh chapter of life.

After around 14 hours of journey, I finally reached Nagpur railway station at 9:00 PM. Even in April, when summer began in India, it wasn't very hot that evening. The air was dry but pleasantly cool. I came out of the station and looked for an auto-rickshaw. Mr Fadnavis had given me his address, and I asked around for the best way to reach Swawlambi Nagar.

His house was on the main road, which was not difficult to find. It was a decently built house named *Parishram* (Hard Work). As I opened the black rot iron gate to enter, I saw a car parked in the driveway leading to the front main door. Lush greenery surrounded the cemented driveway, and the house was engulfed in different trees, which, as I would learn the following day, were Mango and Papaya. I could see the sacred Tulsi at the entrance and roses blooming in the small garden. With nervous excitement, I rang the bell.

A bald, 6-foot-tall man with a fair complexion and a fit body opened the door. He looked like someone who was highly into fitness and exercise. So, this was Milind Fadnavis.

"Hi, I'm Mehul Patel," I introduced myself.

"Welcome to my home, Mehul. Hope you had a good journey," Milind gestured me inside.

"Yes, sir, I did. Thank you," I replied as I entered.

"Why are you so late? Was your train delayed? It was supposed to reach Nagpur at 9 PM, wasn't it? It's almost 11 PM now. By auto, you can reach in 35 minutes or a maximum of 45, considering traffic," asked Milind.

"I- I- I came to Nagpur for the first time, s- so I faced some difficulties while hiring an auto and coming out of the station," I nervously replied.

"*Haan*, that's okay. No issues. I was just worried. Come, come inside," Milind said calmly.

As we entered the house, I crossed a small room to enter a big hall where a tall and slim woman sat with a young child in her lap, trying to make him sleep.

"This is my wife, Saanvi, and my two-year-old son, Shubh," Mr Fadnavis introduced his family.

"Hello, ma'am. I'm Mehul," I said, folding my hands in Namaste.

"Welcome to our home, Mehul. I hope you have a comfortable stay for the next few days," Saanvi welcomed me with a smile as Shubh played on her lap, refusing to sleep.

"Thank you, ma'am," I said sheepishly.

"Please excuse me, Mehul, but this little munchkin is troubling me a lot tonight. It's like he knows that he'll be travelling tomorrow, and that's why he's overexcited," she said as she continued trying to make the fussy baby sleep.

"Yes, Mehul, Saanvi has an early morning flight to Bhopal to her parents' place. It'll be just the two of us over the next three days," explained Milind. "Come, let me show you to your room. It's late now, and we start early in the morning."

I followed Milind to the first floor, where the guest room was and where I would stay for the next three days. The house was modern-looking, with two bedrooms on the ground floor and a kitchen. There was a small pantry on the first floor. The staircase led to the second floor, which I guessed was the terrace.

"There's a small pantry across the lobby, Mehul," said Milind. "There's water and some fruit there, in case you're hungry. I hope you were served dinner on the train."

"Yes, yes, I'm quite full. Thank you, Sir."

"Good, I'll see you at 8.30 AM?"

"Yes, sure, Sir. Good night."

"Good night, Mehul."

I changed into my night clothes, spoke to my parents, and told them I had reached Milind's place safe and sound. As I lay on the bed, I remembered what Amit uncle said about Mr Fadnavis.

"Milind is a creative and self-made person, Mehul. He has turned his passion for training into a thriving consultation business all on his own. He's not one to beat around the bush – he's straight up and honest, which is crucial for his line of work. Like a skilled doctor, he pinpoints his client's issues and helps them out. He's a guru for growing organisations, having learned the ropes through his experiences and meeting with the top people. He's not into comparing people; he truly believes everyone's got their unique journey and challenges. That's what makes him stand out – he's always learning and isn't afraid to admit when he doesn't have all the answers," he had said, and I was looking forward to being mentored by him.

Day - 1

4

*"The first step toward change is awareness.
The second step is acceptance."*

~ Nathaniel Branden

6:00 AM | Attitude of Gratitude

I woke to the phone ringing on my bedside. I didn't realise how tired I was or what time I had slept. I checked my watch; it was 6 AM. The phone on my bedside was an intercom, and Milind was calling me to tell me to wake up and that he was just going to drop his wife and kid at the newly renamed Dr Babasaheb Ambedkar Airport and will be back soon. I should be ready and be there for breakfast at 8:30 AM sharp.

8:30 AM

I felt proud to be punctual as I reached the breakfast table on time. Milind was waiting for me there.

"Good morning, sir," I said.

"Good morning, Mehul. Hope you slept well," Milind asked.

"Yes, sir, I did. Thank you. Has your family left?" I enquired.

"Yes, Mehul. I dropped them off at the airport this morning. They'll be back in a few days," he informed me.

"Okay."

A lady, probably in her mid-50s, came out with a large bowl with steam coming out of it and put it on the table. The aroma was delicious. She then placed some toasted bread on the table.

"Thank you, *Maushi*," Milind said to the lady and then went on to say something in Marathi, which I couldn't understand.

He turned towards me smilingly and said, "Mehul, this is *Maushi*. She cooks for us. I just told her that you will be staying here for the next three days and to feed you some good Marathi dishes."

"Namaste, *Maushi*," I said to the old lady. She smiled at me and quickly left the room.

"Mehul, from now on, you will call me *bhaiya* for the next three days. Is that okay?" Milind said while serving himself some coffee and toast.

"Sir…" I was a little surprised at the sudden request. "I mean, *bhaiya*, sure. I don't mind, but may I know why?"

"Sure, you can ask me as many questions as you want. I don't mind questions being asked! That's what you're here for, isn't it? Please understand this as a lesson for life - I'm trying to get you out of your comfort zone. You have become comfortable in calling me 'sir,' but when you address me as *bhaiya*, it will be a different experience. You can talk to me as you will to your elder brother, your *bhaiya*. You have been calling me "sir" for a few days. I find it very formal. Now, I am telling you, you must start calling me bhaiya," Milind explained.

"Hmm…" I pondered. "Sure, this makes sense, bhaiya."

"Tell me, Mehul," continued Milind, "what do you do once you wake up in the morning?"

"Bhaiya, when I wake up, I usually check my cell phone," I replied sheepishly.

When I graduated, Papa had gifted me a brand-new Nokia 6680. It was a colour-display phone with two cameras—back and front! At Rs. 7,500, it was the most expensive thing I ever got from my father. It was my prized possession. I enjoyed playing games on my phone, especially since 'Snake' was so good in colour. Calls were expensive and for emergencies only.

"Mehul, what do you check on your phone?" Milind asked.

"Umm, if there is any message or missed call from Papa, Mummy, or my friends," I replied with a half-truth. No way was I going to tell him about playing games on my phone.

"In the mornings, I also think about my future plans, career path, what I should do, where I should work…, and those kinds of things," I continued. "At times, I read the newspaper to see what is happening around the country and the world. I sometimes feel I have many problems to solve today, and I play different scenarios in my mind on how to solve them?"

"Okay," Milind stated. "Let me give you a scenario."

"Yes, bhaiya," I focused on listening to what he would say while I put that delicious, aromatic *poha* on my plate, toasted bread, and poured myself a cup of coffee.

"Imagine someone who has been in a state of unconsciousness, whether it's a person waking up after years in a coma or even just yourself after a decade of sleep. What's the first thing you'd think? What would you do? Who would you want to see first?"

"When your mind finally kicks into gear," Milind continued without waiting for a reply. "The first thing most people do is figure out where they are and what's going on. After they understand and the gaps are filled in, it's natural to feel a surge of gratitude—either for life they've been given another chance at or for the wake-up call to start appreciating what they have. This, my friend, is the first step to change.

No matter what you're going through or what challenges you're facing, your mind performs best when you appreciate what you have. Before diving into self-improvement, take a moment to cherish yourself. It's not always easy; I get that. But start by accepting yourself for who you are. Trust me, it's a crucial first step. And to make it a bit smoother, take stock of what you've got right now. Don't tell me you've got nothing – if you've got two working legs and hands or even just a sharp mind, you're already ahead in the game. We often overlook these blessings, but they're the foundation for taking action and moving forward," he concluded.

As Milind talked about different aspects of life, I listened passionately. He was not wrong to say, *'First, see what you have, appreciate it, and only then can you grow by learning different aspects of life.'* I have always been conscious of my stammering, but many people cannot even speak. I should be grateful that I can at least talk.

It was almost 10:16 AM while we were having this discussion, still at the breakfast table.

"Mehul... Let's take a break for 10 minutes. Let me check some business emails. Meanwhile, think about what I said. If you want, you can read the newspaper. It's kept on the coffee table. Till then, identify all that you are thankful for in life and why?" said Milind.

"Yes, Bhaiya," I said, eyeing the newspaper.

5

"Sometimes when you are in a dark place, you think you have been buried, but actually you have been planted."

~ Christine Caine

10:30 AM | No Excuse

When he called my name, I joined him in the small room in the front, which, now in the clarity of the day, looked like his office space with a desk and computer. A whiteboard was hung on one of the walls, and marker pens and a duster were kept beside it. On the wall on the opposite side was a shelf filled with books.

"How was your break, Mehul?" Bhaiya asked when I entered.

"It was good, bhaiya," I replied, sitting on the other side of the desk.

"Okay... You look more relaxed and refreshed. Did something happen in these 10 minutes?"

"No, Bhaiya," I said. "Actually, during the break, I picked up the paper in which the story of a farmer and his struggles was published. Earlier, I thought I had only problems and challenges. But when I read about this farmer, I realised how lucky I was."

"What was the farmer's story?" asked Milind.

"The usual, bhaiya. Every day, we hear about these farmers committing suicide because they have huge debts. They do honest and hard work, yet all their hard work goes in vain if it doesn't rain on time," I said solemnly. "Then I think of how I crib if even small things don't go the way I want. At least my *kismat* is not dependent on the weather conditions. It's in my hands."

"We are indeed lucky. I am not saying farmers are unlucky, but many people have different struggles and work hard to make our lives easy. And we blame our lives. I have a straightforward philosophy for growing," Milind started explaining.

"Whenever you feel depressed about your problems, look at those facing more challenges than you," he continued. "I am not saying you have to compare your challenges with them; you just have to understand that what you face is not impossible. Yes, it may not be easy, but it is possible. If you are looking for a job and feel tense, think of a student who didn't clear exams. They also want to work, but they can't. What do you say to that?"

"You're 100% right, bhaiya," I agreed.

"Whenever you feel you have something more than you need, you have to give to those who need it more than you do. Do you know the secret to living is giving? No matter how empty or broke you are, you always have something to give to others," said Milind.

"But I have one problem," I said. "I.. I.. I feel I am poor at speaking confidently, especially in English. I am from a small city with limited growth options. Very few people speak English in my circle, so I lack the practice."

"Ha ha…" Milind laughed at this. "This is what stopped you from succeeding—this thinking, not your English speaking skills. Whenever you make an excuse, you are preventing yourself from growing. Do you know making excuses is just like someone holding you back from your collar? And the person who is holding you back is none other than your thinking patterns—a big giant 'who' is inside of you."

"As soon as you stop making excuses, you start growing and developing. Once you make excuses, you transfer your responsibility onto another's shoulders for something or the other," continued Milind.

"Let me tell you, people have different excuses. They may have poor language and communication skills, or they have no time, or they're shy, or they can't speak to others. Some even say they're not good-looking – too fat, too thin, or that they're dark-skinned, and many, many more such pretexts. Don't have these types of excuses. The best way to grow in life is to take it all... all means, all responsibilities on your shoulders. It doesn't matter what you do or where you belong… You can make things happen only when you are aware of yourself. But for this, you have to decide that you have to grow. Once you make a decision, you cannot change. You can change your actions and strategy, but you cannot change your decision."

I absorbed everything he was saying.

"Do you know that most people make decisions about so many things and then do nothing about them? For example, you decide one day you want to do business and will be successful in it because you are hardworking and honest. But where you may fail is deciding what business to do according to your interests and aptitude, how much you need to invest, calculating the pros and cons, calculating the return on investment and the time when it'll turn into profit. What I'm trying to say is - to decide about fewer or smaller things and then complete them. Either you do it, or you don't. There are no other options. Have you heard anyone say I am almost married? That means no married person can say that I am practically married. Are you with me, Mehul?" he asked me when I remained silent.

"Yes, bhaiya. But what if a guy like me is unaware of what to do or which area I should focus on first? What should I do… or from where can I start?" I asked.

"Hmm... What are your qualities…What are the top areas in which you are good? Think about this. Do you have answers to these questions? Or have you thought about this?"

"No, not at all."

"Okay. What's the time now?"

I had totally forgotten about the time. I checked my watch, and it was already 1:00 PM.

"It's almost lunchtime. Oh, Sorry. It is lunchtime, not almost," I corrected myself immediately.

"That's right. Let's have lunch and then discuss where to start. Once you finish your lunch, you can relax and think about what we just discussed," said Milind.

"Sure." I was starving. My mind was only on food, not the exercise bhaiya was about to give me.

Milind went to the cabinet on the side and opened a drawer. He searched a few files, picked out some pages, and gave me this one page.

"Mehul," he said. "This is for you to keep you awake after lunch."

He kept the file on the table and rubbed his hands like he was feeling cold, but later, I understood that he was just getting excited.

By the time I freshened up and reached the dining table, Maushi had laid the lunch. She had prepared daal-chawal, chapatis, and Aloo sabzi.

I was worried that at lunch, Milind would ask me about my life, passions, etc. What would I say? How would I reply?

"Mehul, what are you thinking? Take a plate; we have to serve ourselves. No one will come to serve you," he reminded me.

"Yes, Bhaiya."

I took a plate and served myself as we sat for lunch together. Surprisingly, Milind didn't talk about life and goals. Instead, he spoke about food. He asked me how my mother prepared *achar* and what kind of lunch we ate in Vadodara. I guess he was fond of food. He told me about the time he had food at my dad's restaurant and their many discussions over lunch. Thankfully, this topic relaxed my nerves and made me comfortable.

Our lunch was delicious, and once we were done, Milind told me to take a half-hour break and meet him back at 2:00 PM in the front room. I went upstairs to 'my' room with a diary, pen, and the paper Milind had given me before lunch.

I Saw the Paper:

Best Ways to Identify Your Purpose or Passion in Life

(Sample Questions - Use only five which are simple, practical and yet powerful)

- What do you want to do?
- Who you are?
- What You wanted to do?
- Why do you want to do it?
- Think in the best way you want to do it.
- Identify the reasons why you wanted to do it.
- Thoughts in the morning that help you to get up
- Magic of 90 (thoughts you think are the same).
- Things you are attracted to.
- Ask the three people who know you well what you should do.
- Can you define yourself in one word?
- What are your greatest strengths?

- ➤ What are your five weaknesses?
- ➤ Call five people to learn more about your strengths and weaknesses. (These five people may include - Parents, siblings, friends, teacher/mentor, colleagues or professional acquaintances, and other relatives - people who know you)

6

A man who dares to waste one hour of time has not discovered the value of life.

~ Charles Darwin

2:00 PM | The Start

As I sat in my room checking the paper, I started writing on it. Some questions I knew, and others made me think. Maybe I had not thought about some things like this.

At 2:00 PM, I went downstairs. Bhaiya told me to sit and relax and asked me about the exercise.

"I got the answers to the questions, but not completely, especially who I am and my weaknesses," I said.

"Oh, don't worry about it. You have to think and fill it in. It may be possible that it will take you a day to answer them. But don't postpone it until tomorrow. Because what comes to the mind first in a fraction of a second is the final answer. No worries. If you do it today, you will have much time to think and act."

"Bhaiya, I couldn't understand one thing."

"What is it, Mehul?"

"What is the 'Magic of 90?'"

"Hmm… good question, Mehul. The average person has over 60,000 thoughts daily. Of those 60,000 thoughts,

90% are repetitive—throughout the day and from previous days! That's why Magic of 90 - your repetitive thoughts give your life purpose.

"Hmm... interesting. So, what's next, bhaiya?" I asked.

"Take this page and also take a pencil and eraser."

I opened the folded page and found this circle with eight sections prepared. You can choose any of the following areas. You rank the top eight regions.

List of Areas:

- Health
- Education (Education, professional certification)
- Career (Associations and Internships)
- Income (Salary, New income sources, incentives, New ventures)
- Relationships (Self, family, friends, colleagues, society)
- Travel (Holidays, breaks, business tours, unplanned short trips)
- Adventure
- Sports
- Happiness
- Business
- Social Contribution (Volunteering, partnerships, NGOs)

- Help (Juniors, siblings, friends, mentoring)
- Family Time
- Spiritual (Healing, meditation, prayer, yoga)

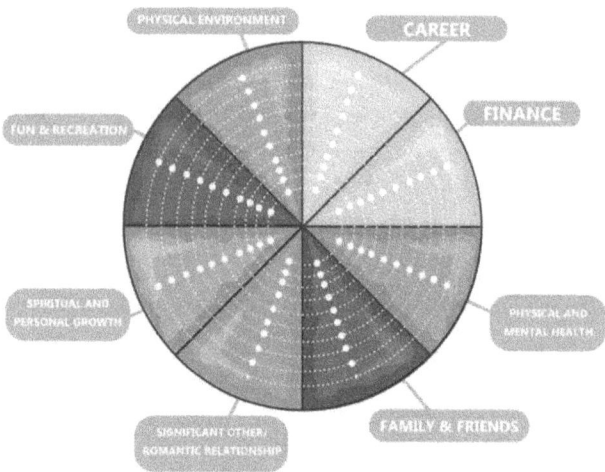

"You have to choose only eight areas, and the circle's centre point represents Zero (0), and the end of the radius represents 10, as shown in the chart," Milind continued. "Now, mark yourself in the following seven areas from 0 to 10. Don't mark anything as 5, as it says nothing. Either 4 or 6. Stop being mediocre."

After listening to Milind, I chose my eight areas, and those were:

Finding The Brand In You

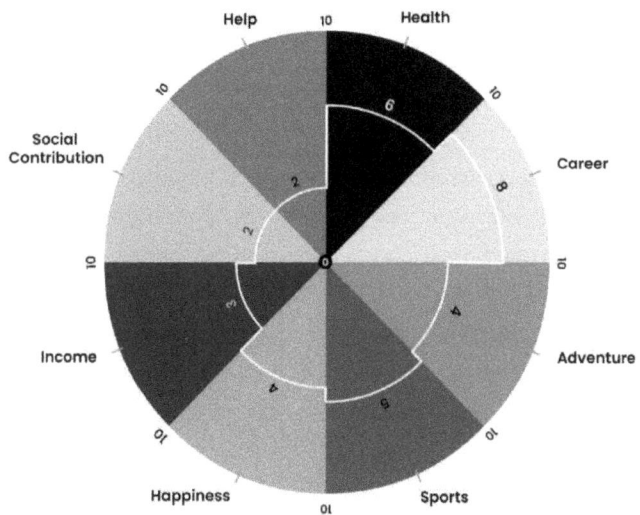

1. Health
2. Career
3. Adventure
4. Sports
5. Happiness
6. Income
7. Social Contribution
8. Help

"Take the next 10 minutes and mark according to you on a scale of 0 to 10. But before that, tell me why you chose these areas step by step?" said Milind.

"Bhaiya, I was not a top-ranked student, but I worked hard. I neglected my health during that process, and my immune system weakened. So, I choose health first," I replied in all sincerity.

"Of course, a career never stops with anyone. It will keep growing, but you must learn through education and experience. So, I chose a career at number two," I continued. "I chose adventure next because although I enjoy visiting my relatives, I also crave adventure. So, I thought, why not combine the two? That way, I get the best of both worlds—family time and thrilling adventures!

I chose sports next because I don't play too much but want to. Happiness comes next. I am not sad, but I overthink a lot and want to be happy. I want to earn a lot of money and become self-made, so I chose income next. To be honest, I do not know about social contribution, but it sounds good, so I chose it. I want to help someone who is in need. I am confused about help and social contributions, bhaiya," I concluded.

"Mehul, you are smart. Even if you don't look smart, you are smart," smiled Milind.

I smiled back. It was the first time somebody appreciated me. I felt terrific about myself.

"What next, Bhaiya?" I asked.

"Start giving ranks; you have the next 10 minutes in hand. Your time starts now," Milind said, looking at his watch.

I started giving ranks, and once I was done, Milind asked me to join the points so that another smaller circle could form.

"Done, bhaiya. But what does it denote?" I asked, confused, looking at the smaller circle.

"The Lowest Ranking means that you have to work more in that area. Here, you ranked Health 1 and Social Contribution 7, so your focus should be on your health. If you make it colourful, it is more clearly visible," Milind explained.

Now, when I saw my circle, I was speechless. It was a shocking experience for me.

"What happened, Mehul? Why are you silent?" asked Milind.

"Bhaiya, I can see which area I lack the most. This exercise is an eye-opener for me. I am worried about my areas. What do I do next, bhaiya?" I asked.

"Ha Ha... Don't worry. Confusion is the first step to clarity. Initially, you were confused about your career. You contacted me, we met, and now you know the areas in which you must work harder. If you rank them in increasing order, you can easily understand the first area where you must work. But remember, this whole exercise is fruitful only when you do it honestly."

"This circle is called the 'Wheel of Life'," continued Milind. "Both the inner circle and the outer circle are visible to you. Your life should be like an outer circle, but your actual life is like an inner circle, and that's why you are unable to balance it. I can see you are getting what I want to say."

"Yes, bhaiya, sure. Now I know where to go, but I still have one doubt."

"Yes?"

"Bhaiya, how do I work on each area?" I asked, scratching my head.

"Do you know someone in excellent health – the area you lack the most? Think," Milind said.

"Let me think… *Haan*, Bhaiya. My uncle's son is a health freak. He regularly goes to the gym and is very conscious of his food and diet," I informed him. "But what should I do with my cousin?"

"Listen carefully to what I am going to say. If you can learn from other people's lives, you are taking advantage of their experience. You are actually converting decades into days. You don't have to reinvent the wheel. You ask and observe your cousin to understand why he is doing what he is doing. You will get answers to all these questions," Milind explained.

"Bhaiya, I can, but I feel you can give me a better answer than my cousin," I said, speaking my mind.

"I don't entirely agree. I want you to work toward your goals. If you identify solutions for growth, you will apply those tools and techniques for a longer time. I am here to solve your problems… reminding you of what I said earlier – if you come here, you will learn more about life than a job. So, I am preparing you for life. So, if you want to know anything, just identify who is doing better than you and get the hint," Milind said.

"Get the hint, from where?" I asked, confused.

"I believe everybody who is doing good in whatever they do leaves some hints or clues about their success. They have some unique thoughts or methods they're using in the field that set them apart," he explained.

"Hmm... Now I get it. You are like Lord Krishna to my Arjuna, bhaiya... Right? You want to guide me to the right path, but I must walk on it alone," I smiled.

"Can we move on?" said Milind, smiling back. "See, Mehul, many people want to do great things but don't know where to start. So, this discussion and exercise will help you find exactly where to start. Now you can see where you are and where you should focus."

"What is the Goal?" I asked.

"What's your biggest dream, Mehul? Think."

"I want a car, a big, shiny black coloured car."

"Which Car?"

"Audi."

"Which Model?"

"Audi - A6"

"By which year do you want to buy this car?"

"By 2012 or maybe 2015."

"Date?"

"How do I know the date?"

"When's your birthday?"

"11th Jan."

"What do you do once you get the car?"

"I will go on a trip with my family, especially my parents."

"Which trip?"

"Maybe a road trip to Goa."

"Maybe or sure, Goa?"

"Goa."

"How will you feel when you go to Goa in your car?" asked Milind.

"Absolute achievement, and thankful to God for making this happen," I said thoughtfully.

"So, here is your goal statement: 'Yes…I feel awesome and thankful to the Almighty while travelling to Goa in my new Black Audi A6 with my parents on 11th January 2015'.

Remember, what we just did was to make you a 'Goal Statement.'

1. Dream + Deadline = Goal. We have a deadline for your goal.

2. We made this sentence in the present continuous tense.

3. We added some feelings.

4. We fixed the date.

5. We fixed everything.

6. If it is helping you to stretch your potential, then it is a Goal." he concluded.

As bhaiya went through the points, I listened intently, though my face showed total surprise.

"What happened, Mehul? Why is your mouth open?"

"Bhaiya, is it really possible? I enjoyed visualising that I was going to Goa."

"Wonderful," said Milind. "That's what's needed to achieve the goal. This is also called the importance of visualisation. If you can see it, you can perceive it."

"So, I just have to keep visualising?"

"No, then you will not get your car," said Milind.

"So, what should I do?" I asked.

"You have to work in reverse engineering. You have to increase your actions to move you towards your goal. Divide your goal into small mini-goals. So, your above-mentioned goals are divided into small actions. Before going for Audi, let's go with a Hyundai or a Maruti. They help you spark your potential. When you achieve small steps, you can easily accomplish the more significant steps. The **Law of Action** is more important than the **Law of Attraction**.

The more actions you take, the faster you reach your goal. But you must learn from your every action, whether helping you move toward your goal or bringing you back. **Do-Learn-Move**. That *funda* of achieving anything in life," he finished saying.

"Got it, Bhaiya," said Mehul. "Now, I aim to wake up tomorrow at 6 AM."

"Mehul, it's not the goal; it's the decision to do it. A goal is something that pushes your limit. Waking up at 6 a.m. may be a decision, but after 6 AM, what you do to help you achieve your goal is important."

"100% agree," I nodded.

"It was a wonderful discussion. Oh, it's already 4:40 PM. Let's have a 10-minute break and then have tea together." Milind said, looking at his watch.

"Sure, Bhaiya, I have so many things to do," I said, rubbing my hands.

"This is the magic of goals. They ignite you to go the extra mile and keep you motivated. As I mentioned, you can work out for different areas of life."

"Yes, we can achieve many things if we know what we want. Clarity gives birth to energy and enthusiasm, which helps us take action," I said excitedly.

7

A Man is great not because he hasn't failed; a man is great because failure hasn't stopped him.

~ Confucius

5:00 PM | Leadership: Seed of Every Action

After a wonderful discussion on goals, I had much more clarity about what I wanted to achieve and was aware of the areas I must work on. But still had doubts about how to start or where to start.

"Mehul, are you ready after the break?"

"Yes, bhaiya."

"Let's go for a walk in the society park."

"Sure, Bhaiya. Let's go."

We left the house and talked about my daily routine and habits. We reached the lovely park with cosy benches for elders and a fun playground for kids. Lush trees, colourful flowers, and happy laughter made it a perfect spot for everyone. Several small vendors set up carts in one corner of the park to attract children. There was a balloon guy, an ice cream vendor, a lemonade and juice vendor, and a guy with small toys like kites, a bow and arrow, etc. It looked like a special area for vendors, close to where the kids played and could easily spot them.

"Ice cream?" Milind asked.

I nodded. Ice cream seemed like a good idea in the blazing summer.

As we were walking towards the ice cream vendor, we saw a little kid of about 5 or 6 years crying because he couldn't find his mom. Milind walked up to him, kneeled, and gently asked if he needed help. He nodded, still crying. Milind bought him an ice cream to calm him down, and then he took his hand and started looking around the park together. After a few minutes, we spotted a worried-looking woman with a toddler in her arms and called out to her. She was the child's mother and had just run after the toddler who decided to follow a 'sparrow' in the park. When she came back and couldn't find the elder son, she panicked and was about to call the cops – when she heard our voice and saw her child. She rushed over and thanked Milind over and over again.

When we left them to get our ice cream, I asked, "Did you know the kid or the mother?"

"Not at all; I saw them for the first time," Milind replied as he paid the ice cream vendor.

"I know it was good of you to help the child, but why did you buy him an ice cream? Kids are told not to take anything from strangers, and sometimes it can be misinterpreted. What if she thought you were kidnapping the child?"

"Mehul, my dear, I was convinced of what I was doing, so I did. That lady didn't say anything to me, which is good, but even if she had said something about getting an ice cream for her child, it wouldn't matter. My intentions were clear. I wanted to help someone, even though I didn't know the outcome."

"Interesting."

"This 'interesting' part is called leadership. Let's discuss it now. How would you define leaders?"

"Umm... Leaders are politicians or guides. You can say they have groups to manage. They are in charge of a group of people."

"Exactly. Everybody thinks in this way, and almost everybody is wrong."

"What!?!" I was astonished at the answer.

"Yes. You are 100% wrong. Let me tell you what leadership is." Milind went on to discuss the importance of leadership, and I listened keenly.

Leadership has five important ingredients:

1. It starts with YOU.

Leadership is how you think, feel, and act. But in society, it has worked in reverse. Let me give you an example. If a small kid starts walking and falls down for some reason, their mom pretends to hit the ground, mockingly hurting it. When the mother 'hurts' the earth, the kid thinks it is the ground's fault, not theirs. Subconsciously, in their mind, a pattern starts forming that whatever happens in our lives is due to others.

You see, for most people, situations and incidents are for good things. The blame is for bad things.

See what we are unconsciously learning: If something terrible happens to me, I blame others, but if something good happens, I take the credit. It's like a man winning a lottery and getting 5 lakh rupees. He says, "Wow, I'm so lucky!"

Good things in my life.   - It is due to me.

Unexpected happening   - It is due to others.

But understand this - whatever happens in your life. It is due to YOU only and no one else.

Milind explained the above with a lot of animation.

"Bhaiya, how can bad things happen to people because of them? I am confused. If somebody has a problem, say, a critical disease, like cancer, how's that person's fault?" I interrupted.

"It's the right question at the right time!" Milind exclaimed. "Mehul, what does it mean if you face problems with your decision? It means you have to learn from your choices. Let me explain. You talk about cancer. Cancer is caused by genetic changes that lead to uncontrolled cell growth and tumour formation. These changes can be caused by a combination of a person's genetic factors and external agents. This means that apart from genes, it could be because of our lifestyle and habits. A smoker has a higher chance of getting lung cancer than a non-smoker. Your diet, your consumption of alcohol and even your age are factors that may lead to different kinds of cancers."

"So, we can control having cancer?" I asked.

"I'm not a doctor, and this is not my area of expertise, Mehul. However, good exercise, a proper diet, a healthy lifestyle, and regular health check-ups can even prevent cancer."

I nodded silently.

"Coming back to what we were discussing," Milind continued, "Problems aren't always what people think they are. If a decision helps you grow in your career, life, or any other area, then it's the right decision. But if a decision stops you from growing, it's not right. Think of it this way: if you face difficulties and challenges with a decision, congratulations—you're on the right track. The right decisions often come with tough challenges at first.

Imagine you bought a house for your parents for 50 lakh rupees, thinking you could arrange all the funds. But you couldn't gather the entire amount due to some emergencies and faced difficulties. Are these really problems? Not at all. This decision helps you strengthen your planning or understand real estate investment better.

Here's how you benefit:
1. You learn how to invest in real estate and what to avoid next time.
2. You gain insight into your decision-making process.
3. You bought a house worth 50 lakh rupees.

You've learned a lot from all these situations. That's my point. Instead of blaming yourself, accept that there might be issues to address. Take responsibility and act on it.

So, always remember that whenever something happens to you or something you want to do, it starts with YOU. Take that responsibility. The faster you take responsibility, the quicker you grow."

"Got it, bhaiya. Now I am responsible for getting a job, and I have to improve on myself."

"Yes, you are. Don't blame anyone. It takes time and focus. Blaming is easy; doing is difficult, so my second ingredient of leadership is action."

Milind continued with the next leadership quality.

2. Initiated Action.

Nothing happens if you don't act. I always tell people that how they think and feel doesn't matter, but what they do matters significantly. You can also say actions speak louder than words.

You have to take the initiative to take action. Just now, you saw me take the initiative to help a child at an ice cream shop.

This is the quality of a leader. They take actions not to inspire others but to inspire themselves. When we take action, we actually help ourselves only. We are curing our fear. **Action Cures Fear.**

It was almost 6:10 PM, and we were walking near the park.

"Let's walk back towards home," Milind said.

I was listening to Milind intently, and everything was sinking in deeply. I wasn't tired, but I was thinking a lot because I had never had so much knowledge in one day. It was really something new.

"What happened, Mehul?"

"Nothing, Bhaiya. I'm thinking about what you just said."

"Okay...Let's walk some more and sit near the fountain."

"Okay, Bhaiya."

While walking, I asked bhaiya if anything important made people leaders other than action and responsibility.

"Yes, That's the third quality of a leader. And that's the hunger to grow."

3. Hunger to Grow.

Leaders always want to grow. It is not about finances or career. They are very hungry to go the extra mile. They want more from themselves all the time. They believe, **"Either You Grow or Die."**

They constantly seek solutions to their problems, so you can also say that leaders are problem solvers. But it should come from inside, not from outside.

Let's say I tell you to meet someone for career advice. You might go, but you might not pay full attention. However, if you decide to go on your own by pushing yourself, you'll learn a lot more. Leaders always push themselves. They break their old records and set new ones. They compete with themselves. If they succeed, they keep improving. If they fail, they still keep going, learning from their mistakes and actions.

Leadership is all about asking for more, going the extra mile, or delivering something more. You can also say that for everything you do, for yourself or others. When you start asking for +1 for yourself, then it is leadership.

Leader finds the way, goes the way, and shows the way. Whether you are a professional or a sportsman, a student or a businessman, everyone needs leadership to progress faster in life.

"Did you understand what I said?" he asked after the explanation.

"Yes, Bhaiya. I get it. I want more, too, and I promise I'll achieve something big in my life."

"Mehul, let me stop you right there. When you achieve something big, you'll need the fourth thing. That's being human."

4. Being Human.

Leadership lessons teach you to be human before achieving something or reaching your life's peak. You have to be more humble, morally correct, and helpful.

Your success should not affect your attitude as you progress towards success in life. You should be more humble and more human. That's the quality of a good leader.

"Now I know the qualities of a leader, but what's the endpoint? For example, what will a leader do once he becomes more humble?" I asked curiously.

"Hmm, interesting. There is no end point for a leader, but once a leader succeeds in his field and people start appreciating them, then remember,

Appreciation = More Responsibility = More Work for the betterment of society.

Your responsibility increases. Responsibility for creating more leaders. And that's our fifth ingredient of leadership."

5. Create More Leaders.

Being a leader isn't just about giving orders or telling people what to do. It's about something deeper. Leaders are like people who light up a room just by walking in. But here's the thing – being a leader isn't just about being in charge. It's about making more leaders.

Imagine you're planting seeds. A leader is like a gardener, scattering seeds of inspiration and knowledge wherever they go. But here's the trick – before you can teach others, you've got to know your stuff. It's like saying, 'Don't just talk the talk; walk the walk.'

You help someone out with what they need. Maybe it's advice, a helping hand, or just a friendly ear. And guess what? By doing that, you're actually helping yourself too. It's like magic! That's the secret sauce of a true leader – helping others without expecting anything in return.

And here's where it gets even better. When you help someone who can't repay you, that's when the real magic happens. It's like discovering this superpower of giving without expecting anything back. And you know what that brings? Happiness. Not just any old happiness, but the kind that spreads like sunshine.

But wait, there's more. See, leaders aren't just single players. They're like community builders, crafting a web of good people around them. Because when you've got a bunch of good people helping each other out, that's when the real change happens. That's when you start to see leaders popping up all over the place, making the world a better, brighter, and more awesome place to be.

So yeah, next time you think about being a leader, remember – it's not about being the boss. It's about being the spark that ignites a fire in others. It's about creating a ripple effect of kindness and inspiration that spreads far and wide. Remember, we've all got a little leader inside us, just waiting to shine.

Saying this, Milind looked at the Sky. We were sitting near the fountain in the late evening, and it was getting darker.

I was lost in my thoughts. I had never thought life could be like this. We can leave our mark in society. We can be helpful to someone. I always thought I needed help, but now I felt I had to help more. Suddenly, I felt really refreshed, like all my tiredness disappeared on its own. I felt alive and full of energy. My heart was pounding with excitement as if I had found the secret to life. I glanced at Milind, who was still looking up at the sky.

Suddenly, he turned towards me. "Mehul, when you begin to help others and share what you have, your life's meaning becomes more apparent. You find answers to your questions and feel like you're being drawn towards your purpose instead of having to force yourself. It's like being pulled by something greater than yourself. Many people have dreams that are much bigger than they are, and those dreams can pull you forward with incredible strength. Then, you start living for others, and that's what life is all about. That's the message of life.

The Magic of Living is in Giving.

It is not necessary to start giving when you have something in life. You can begin to give when you have nothing in life. From now on, you can give your time to small children who want to learn something.

But if you want to give more, you have to grow more yourself. That's what leadership is all about. Being a leader means you can steer your own ship, guiding your own life. So, if you want to lead others, start by leading your own life. This is the key factor that directly impacts your personal growth.

I nodded.

"Ice cream, Ice cream..." I heard a vendor calling. Milind bought us two more ice creams.

I felt like a different person altogether. Although I came here to learn how to look for a job, I realised then that I have a bigger purpose and a mission on this earth. I didn't understand what it was then, but I knew I would figure it out soon and was determined to search for it. This thought, combined with my ice cream, made for an incredible feeling. I'd never tasted such sweetness in ice cream before.

By the time we both stood up and walked towards the house, it was 7.45 PM. We spoke little during the short walk; there was much going on in my mind—so much to think about and reflect upon. As we reached home, bhaiya told me to freshen up and meet for dinner at 8.30 PM.

When I reached downstairs, the dinner table was laid. *Maushi* had made some typical Maharashtrian food that I had never heard of, even though my father owned a restaurant back home. I enjoyed Katachi Amti Dal with Puran Polis and some rice. For dessert, there was Orange burfi, a Nagpur speciality.

I felt really fresh, energetic, and relaxed. Despite learning many new things on the first day, chatting with Milind was a pleasure. My mind and body were active, and I felt more responsible for my actions.

After dessert, Milind suggested I review what I learned before going to sleep and asked if we could meet early in the morning. He wanted to meet sharp at 6:00 AM in the front garden of the house. I agreed and checked my watch. It was 9:37 PM. I left for my room while Milind started reading something.

Once in the room, I fell on the bed and stared at the ceiling fan, thinking about my life's purpose. I reviewed everything I had learned during the day and felt more clear about what I wanted and how to achieve it. I asked myself these two questions again and again: What did I want from life, and how would I achieve it? Although the questions kept me awake, I definitely felt better than I had yesterday or in many days.

Manish Upadhyay

Day - 2

8

"Morning is an important time of day because how you spend your morning can often tell you what kind of day you are going to have."

– Lemony Snicket

6:10 AM | Morning Rituals

It was early for me, as I had never woken up so early at home. I walked down to the ground floor in my tracksuit, thinking Milind would start his session early in the morning.

"Bhaiya... Bhaiya," I started looking for and calling Milind.

"Good morning, Mehul."

I heard his voice coming from outside. I had forgotten that he had asked me to go to the garden in the morning. I ran towards it. As I reached the garden, I saw Milind sitting in a yoga position on the grass.

"Come and Sit, Mehul."

"On the Grass?" I asked

"Yes. What's wrong with sitting on the grass?"

"No, nothing. Sure." I sat on the grass.

"How are you? Did you sleep well last night?"

"Yeah, surprisingly, I had a sound sleep. I woke up automatically at around 4:00 AM and then at 5:10 AM, which generally doesn't happen with me. I was surprised, as I'm not an early-morning person. But then I thought it was because you asked me to meet at 6:00 AM. Maybe that's why," I said.

"Signs are good," he said calmly.

"What... what signs?"

"The signs that your brain has started working, and when our brains start working, we become conscious and aware of ourselves," Milind explained.

"Maybe. That's why I woke up early," I murmured to myself.

"Mehul, I asked you to come early in the morning. You see, mornings have a significant role in our lives," he started explaining. "If you ask me what makes 'Achievers, Titans, and Gladiators' different, I'd say it's their routines. They are the ones who don't run away from life's battles. They face and fight with whatever resources they have. Winning or losing doesn't matter; what matters is that they stood up, fought, and broke their own records. They are driven by a hunger for action and progress. They find solutions to problems because they believe in themselves and the hard work they've put in."

I listened carefully.

"This titan breed plans their mornings to engage their minds and give their brains the fuel they need. This morning boost helps them stay sharp all day. So, today,

I'll share the 20:20:20 formula for your morning routine," Milind said.

"What is that?" Immediately, my mind wandered to the 20-20 cricket matches that had recently been introduced in the world of cricket. I had never heard about 20:20:20.

"It is a life game, and it is represented by 20:20:20. If you divide an hour, for the first 20 minutes - you plan and read or write in your journal."

"What is this journal bhaiya?" I asked Milind. Obviously, I knew what a journal was, but I didn't have one of my own.

"A journal is a diary or notebook where you write everything about your life. This diary contains your thoughts, aspirations, goals, planning, knowledge series, wishes and wants series, dreams, and learnings. It is a guide showcasing where you are and where you want to go. In this journal, you can also mention your mentors and heroes, their quotes, inspirational life stories, pictures, etc. In brief, whenever you open your journal, you should feel good and grateful about your life. At the same time, you should have the energy and power to do more and serve more."

"Hmm… I never thought we could prepare such a type of notebook or diary," I mused.

"The message is clear, Mehul. Whenever we write, see, and feel about our goals, we can achieve them."

"Okay…" I said, still deep in thought.

"The first 20 minutes, you will give it to your journal. You will just turn the pages, read, and write. Now we come to the next 20 Minutes. Do some exercise and warm-ups. You can also jog or walk. But you have to move your body. You have to do some power exercises where you get tired and sit down. Are you with me so far, Mehul?"

"Yes, yes, bhaiya."

"Now we come to the last 20 Minutes. Take a seat, close your eyes and sit in the 'Lotus' position. Just be with yourself by closing your eyes. You can sit somewhere you won't get too much outside noise."

"Okay, bhaiya."

"Just check what's going on in your mind. What are your thoughts? Don't analyse whether they're right or wrong; just BE AWARE of what's happening in your head. Ultimately, feel grateful for what you have right now by opening your arms, just like you want a big hug. This all should be done by closing your eyes. This activity helps you become more aware of yourself.

Keep these things in mind while using the 20:20:20 tool:

- It would be great if you were alone for all 60 minutes.
- If it's not possible for 60 minutes, then the first and last 20 Minutes must be done alone.
- Spend these 60 minutes in a place with minimal disturbance.
- You can take a break on Sunday and enjoy your time.
- Make sure you do this at least six days a week.

Once you complete this 20:20:20 activity, you must be with your family for the next 15 to 20 minutes. Give time to your mummy, papa, and loved ones. Be with them. You don't need to talk to them in the morning, but you must spend time with them.

Once you do all the above, you are ready for the world to combat and fight for your dreams."

"Hmm…" is all I could say.

"These are what I call 'Morning Rituals'." Milind continued. "These rituals help you build mental and physical strength. You don't require too much physical strength to fight for your dream; you need excessive mental strength. Develop your mind for the game of life, and only then can you become a strong player."

"What if I cannot take 60 minutes daily, bhaiya?"

"If you cannot take 60 minutes daily, try 30 minutes. However, 30 minutes will only work if you practice the 20:20:20 tool (or 10:10:10 in case of 30 minutes) enough to become an expert in your ritual. You are not living a life if you cannot take out even 30 minutes from your life for yourself," Milind said firmly.

That was a powerful statement. The idea struck me like a hard ball hitting a wall.

"But I have a question," I said.

"Yes?"

"Bhaiya, I don't usually like to do anything in the morning. I just want to sit on a chair, read the newspaper or watch TV. So, what if I don't like these morning rituals?"

"You don't get an option here, Mehul."

"What, Bhaiya... How come?"

"Listen carefully, Mehul. Winners don't enjoy morning routines either, but they stick to them. They know that doing what they don't like can bring powerful results, while doing what they like might not be as effective."

"Umm... I don't get it, bhaiya," I said, confused and scratching his head.

"Let me give you an example. People don't like to eat bitter gourd, *Karela*. Why? They find it too bitter. But if they eat it, they know it helps to clean up the body. It is rich in fibre, controls blood sugar levels, and is good for digestion. Similarly, people like sugary things... it leaves a good taste in their mouth! But what do you get from eating too much sugar?"

"Sugar problem?"

"Yes, diabetes. The point I'm trying to make here is that to win the game of life, you have to do things that you may not like. That's what creates winners! They do what they don't like compared to all the others. People who do not do what they don't like stay behind in the game of life. However, winners do what they don't like, and it uplifts them.

"Hmm..." I pondered.

"*Achcha*, tell me, have you heard of Andre Agassi?"

"Yes, the tennis player."

"Yes. Did you know that Agassi did not like tennis as a kid?" he said.

"He didn't?" I was surprised.

"Yes, he admits this in his autobiography. He hated tennis because it was forced on him. According to Andre, his father wanted one of his kids to be a great tennis player. He tried with the older siblings first and then focused on Andre, who had talent.

When Andre was young, his father took him to the hotels on the Vegas strip to play tennis against rich men. Andre would lose the first set deliberately and then win the next when the stakes were higher, making money for his father.

His father was very strict, and Andre spent hours every day on the tennis court, hitting balls. Andre had no choice as a child, and he hated the game. His rebellious streak came from this hatred. However, despite his resentment, he knew deep down he was good at tennis and kept training. It wasn't until he was an adult that he started to enjoy and take the game seriously. We all know the end result—we have a champion!"

"Yes!"

"Mehul, these people, I call them the titan breed. They make themselves and their mindset so strong that nothing can stop them from achieving what they want. They make their luck daily in the morning. Imagine if you skip your morning routine and dive straight into the day, exposed to a barrage of information from all corners. It's like being thrown into the deep end of a pool without your swimming gear. You will be pissed off, frustrated, and tired of what's happening, and in the end, you will live a mediocre life."

"Point, bhaiya."

"So, when you wake up every morning, take time for yourself. Plan your day and let yourself drive the day rather than let the day drive you."

"Sure. Now I understand why our *rishi muni* and monks woke up early."

"Morning has blessings in itself. It not only gives you hope but also heals your mind and body, allowing you to fight back and bounce back with an increased oxygen supply if you are in the right place. Make your morning, Mehul, my dear friend."

"Sure, Bhaiya."

"What's the time?" asked Milind suddenly.

"It's 7:16 AM."

"Okay… let's go jogging. We will meet back at 8:30 AM at our breakfast table. Anyway, I have one surprise for you."

"Yes, bhaiya. But what is the surprise?"

"Let's run. You go to Fountain Way, and I will run to Temple Way. Both will return soon, and we will meet at 8:30 AM at the breakfast table. Okay?"

"Yes, sir."

I started jogging and thinking about my morning route and that surprise. Anyway, I gave it all to my jogging.

9

"A Man who fears to suffer is already suffering from what he fears."

~ Montaigne

8:30 AM | Action Cures Fear

When I returned home from jogging, I took a long shower. Today, I felt so fresh. I was more active and focused. Lots of energy was bubbling in me, wanting to come out. So, I got ready and reached the breakfast table. Milind was already there.

"Hi, bhaiya. I am ready for breakfast."

"Hello again, Mehul. How was the run? How are you feeling?" asked Milind while serving himself breakfast of Idli, Sambhar and Upma. I served breakfast for myself, too. As we ate, I said, "It was awesome. I am feeling great and energetic."

"Very good, so, what next?"

"Yeah, I was also thinking the same," said Mehul.

"Mehul, we have created acceleration in your engine—your body—now it's time to move that engine, which means starting a task necessary for you. You are searching for a job, right? So, what is important for you? Prepare the resume, apply to multiple companies, and talk to HR managers—these kinds of things, right?"

"Yes, bhaiya. But…"

"But, what?"

"Bhaiya, I.. I don't have the confidence to talk with HR or to meet someone new for my job. When I start speaking with someone new, I forget my name and the message I want to communicate."

"Hmm… I have a question for you, Mehul."

"Yes, bhaiya?"

"Do you lack confidence, or are you afraid?"

"I- I- I think both," suddenly I got nervous.

"Don't say both because both are different. When you do certain things the first time, everyone has that uncomfortable feeling about them. It is called fear, not less confidence. You automatically start losing your fears once you start doing this activity regularly. You become confident. This means that whenever we do something new for the first time, we fear what will happen and how it will be done. Everyone has that feeling. But many people don't try new things just because they are afraid, and they say they lack confidence."

"This means I do not have less confidence; I am having fear?"

"Yes, let me ask you—when did you last talk to a stranger about your job?"

"No one, except you."

"Then how do you know you have less confidence?"

"Hmm... Point. I feel timid when speaking to new people, especially for my job. I don't like to be talked about because of the stammer in my voice, so I feel down."

"See Mehul, first of all, congratulations that you are feeling this way."

"Bhaiya, are you kidding me? I just told you that I sta.. stammer because of n.. nervousness, and I.. I.. I f.. fear connecting with new people, and you are congratulating me!" I said agitatedly.

"No, Mehul, I am not kidding. I am not saying congratulations on your fears. I am congratulating you on your consciousness and awareness. This means you are aware that you are afraid of this. Do you think I didn't notice that you stammered at times, especially when you're nervous? But I'm congratulating you because you are conscious and aware of it, and I can see that you have worked very hard on yourself and your speech issues. You knew where you lacked, and you worked hard to overcome it. So, congratulations," he patted me on my back.

"Thank you, bhaiya," I barely could speak. I was numb and grateful. He understood my issues, and not once did he speak about it. I had grown up being teased about it, and here this man, not only did he not say anything about my issues, but he, in fact, understood all my hard work and appreciated it. No one, not even my parents, understood it. They used to fill the gaps where he would stammer - and it used to hurt him. He knew they meant well - but it felt to him like his self-confidence was being taken away from him. The fact that Milind never completed his sentences and accepted the way he was by letting him finish his sentences, even when he took his time to do so - mattered to him most.

"Until and unless we don't know where we are lacking, how can we grow?" Milind spoke, understanding his silence and not wanting to overwhelm him further. "Unlike you, most people aren't aware of what or where they lack. Some are aware but don't accept it. They feel they will not be treated well if they share their issues with someone or open up with family or friends. Remember, we also did the same thing in the goal-setting activity, where you identified the areas where you have to work and how to get things or take guidance. That's what I liked about you. Even on that first phone call, I could hear your resilience, and that's why I invited you here," Milind told me.

"Thank you, bhaiya," I repeated for the lack of words.

"In your case, you may fear that you will be rejected or not receive the answer you expected. What if:

→ If somebody doesn't like my ideas?

→ If somebody doesn't guide me?

→ If somebody laughs at me?

→ If somebody says that I do not know about particular areas?

Don't these thoughts cross your mind?" he asked.

"Yes. Exactly," agreed Mehul.

"So what? What will happen if things don't happen according to your conditions or requirements? Give me an answer to this – Can we control other people? Their thoughts? Any event? Someone's speech or behaviour, or even their actions?

"No, we can't," Mehul murmured.

"Until and unless an individual is ready to take charge of himself, things will remain the same. Remember, as I said earlier, your father makes key decisions, but you are only responsible for taking action. But people fail here just for two/three reasons:

1. They don't try or take action, thinking that they will fail or get rejected.
2. They want to make everyone happy.
3. They want to do everything perfectly.

When you focus on this, you cannot make progress in life. You cannot make everyone happy. If you are doing that, you are making one person unhappy, and that is you."

"So, what's the solution?" I was curious.

"The solution is simple," Milind replied. "Think of this in points:

1. If you fear something new, ACCEPT it; it's okay to have fear. Change this word to excitement.
2. Now, we will say we feel excited about new actions and paths.
3. Start doing rather than thinking. People have a problem with 'paralysis of analysis'; they

overthink before doing, and overthinking can paralyse you.
4. Once you start doing it, learn from every action and check the results. Nobody can stop you from growing if you can learn from every action you perform.

Let me again give you an example: If you start speaking to new people and they don't respond well, you don't have to stop and think about your luck. Instead, you can consider why they responded to you in this way. What was missing from your side? Think about what new approach you can adopt next time.

Apply this concept in your next interview. If you succeed, good. Otherwise, keep learning from the second one and apply it in the third and henceforth. One day, you will master speaking and connecting with people. Here, we can simply reduce our efforts. We can get help from people who are good at this or try to learn fast from other experts so that it reduces our time, energy, and effort. I am not saying you can learn from experts without actually doing anything," Milind continued.

"I'm sure by now you know how I love to give examples… so here's another one. Think of it this way: You cannot learn to swim by reading books and receiving expert training. You have to jump in the water. Of course, the training and advice will be incredible if you use them while jumping into the water.

Your Actions = Learning from your last actions + Expert Suggestions.

This equation should be run in a closed loop until and unless you reach the point where you are a master in that area. For you, this is speaking to new people. Now, I am playing the role of expert. This is a prerequisite; training will be useless if you do not apply it."

I nodded in agreement.

"I define confidence as when you become a master in your field, that is, whatever field you want to grow in. You will be confident," he continued. "If you ask an expert like a salesman who is confident in selling - why he is confident, he will say that he closed the deal faster than anyone else. And if you ask how he does it, he will share how he grew up. At the micro level, everyone starts from zero, but they learn and grow.

The issue is that people tend to give up pretty quickly, usually after a couple of tries, and then they're like, "Oh, I'm just not cut out for this." I come across many professionals who feel they're not great at public speaking. So, I ask them, "Hey, how many times have you actually tried speaking on stage?" And they're like, "Oh, just two or three times." Then, I ask them why they think they're not making progress. And if they try to tell me they've tried everything, I'm like, "Come on, seriously? If you've genuinely tried everything, you'd have seen some results by now because other people are getting results, right?"

I kept on listening intently.

"So, Mehul," continued Milind. "Who will speak on your behalf about your job if you are afraid of speaking for yourself?"

"Me, bhaiya, I have to talk."

"If you fail and don't get results, what will you do?"

"I will learn and analyse critically what went wrong and improve myself."

"Well, said. If you do this all your life in every aspect, then you become the master of your own life."

Having said that, Milind sat down to drink water. After breakfast, he continuously spoke. I observed that he had become more aggressive since yesterday. His voice had become louder, and he was more action-oriented.

I felt that an army chief was training his commander for a battle, and I was ready for the battle of my life. I never saw my life, actions, fears and results in such a way.

"Any questions, Mehul?" he asked.

"Yes, bhaiya. I've seen people laugh at me if I try something new or say something about people who do something new in society. In our school, a guy named Jignesh brought a science game to help everyone learn new concepts. Unfortunately, no one seemed interested. A few students played with him, but most didn't. Some teachers even laughed at or scolded him for bringing a game to school. Jignesh was smart but didn't get the support he needed. So, what can you do in a situation like that?

"Where is Jignesh right now?"

"What?"

"I asked, what is Jignesh doing nowadays?"

"He is an IIT-ian. He just graduated from IIT- Mumbai."

"Got the answer?"

"No, not exactly," I was confused.

"See Mehul, we live in a society where you will get all kinds of people. Now you have to decide which type of people to live with."

"Which type of people? I mean, how do you decide?" I asked.

"Anyone whose company and thoughts push you towards your goal is the right company. Anyone who pulls you away from your goal is not your company. Get the message? If, say, Ritesh is a new friend in the organisation where you want to work. Ritesh goes to a party and spends too much money there. If that's what you want from your life, Ritesh is the perfect choice, but if not, then leave Ritesh and move ahead. And if people laugh at your actions... then again, congratulations, my dear Mehul. You are growing. People laugh at those who show them what they can't do."

I nodded in agreement.

"These are the signs that you are growing. These things should not affect you or your actions," continued Milind. "However, if criticism comes from your loved ones, just listen carefully and see what you can do about it. Work on it, learn from it, and start doing it. Got it?"

Milind picked up a few cashew nuts and smiled as he munched them.

I thought this man understood life. He was so passionate about helping. I was both surprised and happy at the time. I was surprised because I had never thought about friends and associations this way, and I was delighted that I got the answer about my actions, fear, and confidence to face somebody who made fun of me.

I was so happy, as if I found a precious stone. I laid back on the sofa in the hall, my legs stretched and both my hands behind my head, and started thinking. I looked at bhaiya; he was checking the time. It was 11:00 AM.

"Let's take a 10-minute break, Mehul. Then we'll meet back here."

Bhaiya stood up and went to the office room to check mail and do some office work. Today, I wouldn't say I liked a break; I thought bhaiya should keep sharing his wisdom.

I just opened my diary and wrote:

There are two golden rules for building confidence:

1. Just do it, and
2. It is okay to fail. *Haarna achcha hota hai.*

10

"Nothing in life is more important than the ability to communicate effectively."

~ Gerald R. Ford

11:15 AM | Communication

At around 11:15 AM, I entered the small room in the front of the house - In my mind, I called it the training room.

Before we could start the next topic, the doorbell rang. Milind went to open the door and saw one sales executive come to sell some books. He asked him to come inside, which he did. Milind asked him if he wanted water. He nodded with a grateful smile.

As he drank the water, he scanned the room and saw the vast bookshelf on the wall. He thanked Milind for the water and said, "Thank you, sir. My name is Nivant Thakre. I sell dictionaries. And I need just 10 minutes of your time."

"Yes, tell me, how can I help you, Mr Thakre?" asked Milind.

He cleared his throat and started speaking. "I am sure you have a dictionary at home, and you know its importance. Looking around, I can confidently say you do a lot of reading. It is possible that most people at your home read books."

'Very True," said Milind, making eye contact with him.

"So, I feel," continued Nivant, "you don't need a dictionary. I'm sure you already have one. But sir, if you want to gift someone books or inculcate a hobby of reading, you must think that that individual should have a dictionary to understand the meaning of words. If somebody doesn't understand English words, they skip that portion."

"So, what's your point? What should I do?" Milind asked.

"Sir, my point is simple. Imagine giving a dictionary to someone who wants to develop a reading habit. With a dictionary at their disposal, they can improve their English significantly. You've provided a solution for a common problem readers face, so they'll appreciate and use it.

Our company has an offer for people like you who value books and dictionaries. If you buy one, you get another one for free. One is an English-to-English dictionary, and the other is an English-to-Hindi dictionary. The price for one is Rs. 850, and you get the second one free! Sir, would you be interested in this purchase?"

At first, Milind smiled. He took out his wallet, gave him Rs. 850, and bought two dictionaries. The salesman thanked him and asked for his references for prospective clients. Milind nodded and gave him a couple of references.

As soon as the salesman left, I said, "Bhaiya, I think the dictionaries were costly."

"I know."

"Are these helpful?"

"Yes, they are."

"Why did you buy them at this price from this guy?"

"That's the right question. Very good. This guy, Nivant, came here to sell his dictionaries. I bought them from him for only three reasons:

1. He sold himself without selling himself: He came and behaved according to the person in front of him. He presented himself in a simple, honest, and smart manner.

2. He sold need, not the product: He looked around and understood, due to the presence of mind, that I didn't really need dictionaries. But he found the gap between what people like me generally face. It is true that if I tell someone to develop their English language skills, he will surely do so.

3. He communicated flawlessly: He spoke clearly without jargon or hi-fi language. He kept everything simple, straight, and to the point, which I quickly understood. He didn't beat around the bush, you know? He came straight to the point and seemed confident.

The ultimate thing is that he was focused on the results. He never moved away from the end goal. That's why I bought dictionaries from him. Although costly, the extra cost was a gift to Nivant Thakre. I believe we don't sell our products; we sell ourselves, and Nivant sold himself well. He will achieve greater heights because he knows what to say when," Milind explained.

Bhaiya smiled, looking at my stunned expression while listening to him. I never thought of it this way.

"Bhaiya... so what's the learning for me from this incident?"

"Communication…that's the learning for you. What do you think communication is, Mehul?"

"Communication. Yes, I know. It is how we speak and all."

"That's the biggest mistake you are making. Mehul, communication is not only about speaking; it is much more than that."

"How do you mean?"

"So, you just said communication is all about speaking, right?"

"Yes."

"What about listening? Do you think that is a part of communication?"

"Umm... yes, I guess so. Not sure."

"So, tell me… if you speak to me, and I do not listen to you… would you be able to communicate with me?"

"No."

"Exactly. There's more to communication than just speaking. Okay, tell me, if I ask you to give a percentage to reading, writing, listening, and speaking as part of good communication, how much would you give to each category?"

"I will give 50% to speaking, 30% to reading, 20% to writing and 10% to listening."

"Very good, but sorry to say, you are wrong," Milind said.

I was confused.

He continued, "Have you seen that communication is more difficult when listening than speaking? You have good communication skills if you can listen more and talk less. Nowadays, people have minimal listening ability. They just want to speak. Everyone should talk. Talking is not a problem, but some people don't know when and what to say. That's the problem. Due to this, everything seems difficult or becomes difficult."

"Hmm..."

"Think in this way. Do you know Salman Khan?"

"Yes. I like him."

"Which movies have you seen recently?"

"I have seen every Salman Khan movie, including *Hum Aapke Hain Koun, Tere Naam, Mujhse Shaadi Karogi,* and *Hum Tumhare Hain Sanam.*"

"Very Good. Can you explain why Salman Khan's movie *Tere Naam* was a bigger hit than *Hum Tumhare Hain Sanam*? Although many factors are involved, what is the one thing that makes any movie hit or flop?"

"Maybe because of the poor songs or the film's promotion?" I replied thoughtfully.

"No, Mehul. Any movie becomes a hit or flop when the audience can understand the story. The film becomes a hit if people can connect with the story. If they don't understand the message the movie wants to give, then the movie becomes a flop.

The director designed and created his message. If that message resonates with people or strikes a chord with those who can relate, the movie will succeed. Audiences see their own struggles reflected in the hero's journey. They feel like the hero is one of them. This connection is the key factor that determines whether a movie becomes a hit or a flop," Milind explained.

I listened carefully.

"The same rule applies to communication," continued Milind. "I am not sharing the dictionary meaning of communication. What I'm trying to say is from my experience. If other people understand your message, then your communication skills are good. If people do not understand your message, then communication is weak. Now, it depends on how you communicate your message. You can use hi-fi language, body language, or proverbs—anything to convey the message. Do you like cricket, Mehul?" Milind suddenly asked.

"Yes, bhaiya! Who doesn't?" Mehul smirked.

"In cricket, a batsman hits 6 or 4 runs; how does the umpire communicate a message to the public at the stadium?

"The umpire signals a four or a six with his hands," Mehul said.

"Exactly. The umpire doesn't have to shout. He communicates through hand gestures, that is, through his body language. The intention is obvious: people should be aware of the runs the batsman scored, not about his speaking skills.

We have to follow the same objective in terms of communication skills. So, whenever you want to communicate, remember these three golden rules:

Rule 1: With whom are you speaking?

Rule 2: What do you want to communicate? (Information/ Knowledge/ Facts/Agenda?)

Rule 3: If you will be at their place, what type of communication do you expect?

These three rules will help you understand more about communication and through which you will not face difficulty in communicating with anyone."

"Wow, this is a very new concept," I was excited. "I never thought of it from this point of view. Bhaiya, I have a question—If somebody doesn't know a language or is weak in a particular language, how should that person talk to another person? Say, if I go to Tamil Nadu, and I don't know Tamil, and the other person doesn't know any other language but Tamil, how do we communicate?"

"Brilliant question. See, Mehul, the more you communicate in simple language, the more people admire you. That's the strategy of communication. You should always know the 'outcome' you expect from communication. But when anybody doesn't know English or another language…" He stopped mid-sentence and then asked me, "Hmm, ok, tell me something, Mehul. Have you ever seen your father get angry?"

"Yes, bhaiya, but what is the connection between language and my father's anger?

"Just give me an answer… yes or no."

"Many times. When he gets angry, no one else dares to speak even for a moment in our home."

"Ok. But how do you know your father is angry?"

"His facial expressions change. When he comes home and is angry about something, he smiles less. The pitch of his voice increases not only with us but in everything he says."

"Good observation, Mehul. You know he's angry, even before he utters a word. How?"

"Umm... just by looking at him?"

"Yes. Mehul, you observed his body language—his expressions, maybe his walk, the pitch of his voice, as you said, maybe his walk, and his hand movements. They all change, don't they?"

"Yes, bhaiya."

"Now, can you tell me how much weight body language has in your total communication process? Let's say I have 100%. How much weight should we give body language, tone, and what you actually say?

"Bhaiya, wild guess, right?"

"Yes. Guess?"

"I think body language should be 35% and the rest equally."

"Check this out," Milind gave me a paper with a diagram.

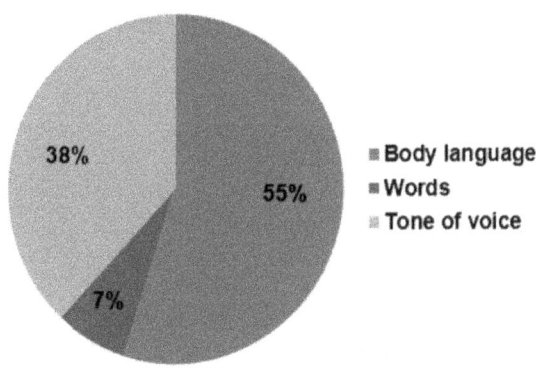

"This is called the Mehrabian formula. Surprisingly, your words and language knowledge only carry 7% weight. This means your words and language are important, but you should not be worried about them. Imagine how people who don't have a voice communicate. They speak with their hand movements. They are also communicating. People who don't speak English keep thinking their English will be good one day, and then they can talk confidently. You should start speaking, and simultaneously, you should develop your communication skills. Focus more on your body language when you have weak language skills."

"You're right, bhaiya. I never thought about it this way! How many times have I seen my father just give me a stare when he's angry at me? Or my mother simply hugs me if I'm upset without telling her I'm upset! I guess she sees my body language too."

"Exactly, Mehul. Do you want to learn more about body language?"

"Yes, Bhaiya… let's do it."

12:30 PM | Body Language

"Before we start, do you have any questions so far, Mehul?" inquired Milind.

"No, bhaiya. I'm good. I need to learn more about body language; it sounds fantastic," I said, rubbing my palms.

"Great. You seem excited! You know how I know - the way you're rubbing your palms. You're giving me signals through your body about what is going on in your mind."

"That's true, bhaiya. I never thought of noticing the body language, or even if I did, I didn't think twice about it," I replied thoughtfully.

"Ok, tell me, Mehul, why is body language needed? Why is it important?"

"Ugh, well, to get to know a person?" I asked, a bit confused.

"Sure, but tell me, have you observed that when you meet a random stranger, your mind gives you a signal about this person? Call it a vibe. You get a vibe from a certain person just by looking at or meeting them randomly – from their dress or appearance or how they move or speak. You make that perception of the individual in your mind. Right?"

"Yes, bhaiya."

"I feel that this is a perception-driven world. Wherever I go, people will make a perception of me – which can either be right or completely wrong. Like, when I go for training, someone may look at me and think – this person looks serious, and the session will be boring. But then I would create a fun activity or share a random joke here and there in training – so that the individual would realise that his initial perception of me was incorrect. And from there on, the perception changes. So, what I believe is – whether we want it or not, people will have perceptions about us. So, why not create a perception right from the beginning?"

"How do you create the perception, bhaiya?"

"Do you know the 3-second rule of communication?"

"No."

"When you're talking with someone, wait about three seconds to respond when they finish speaking. This short pause shows you're listening and gives you a moment to think before you speak. For example, if a friend says, 'I had a tough day at work,' take a brief pause before replying with something like, 'Oh no, what happened?' It makes the conversation feel more thoughtful and respectful. That's the 3-second rule of verbal communication.

The 3-second rule of body language is about holding eye contact for around three seconds before looking away. This helps you appear confident and interested without seeming intense or staring. For instance, if you're meeting someone new, look them in the eyes for three seconds while shaking hands, then briefly look away. This balance makes you seem friendly and attentive, creating a positive first impression. If you do it for over 3 seconds, make eye contact or even give a handshake, it becomes awkward. Are you getting it, Mehul?"

"Yes, Bhaiya. It's interesting."

"Remember, you asked about creating perception. Here are some common things to work on your body language:

- **Stand:** Stand straight on both legs. Many people don't stand straight. They put their body weight on one leg more than the other so that one leg looks smaller and the other appears bigger.

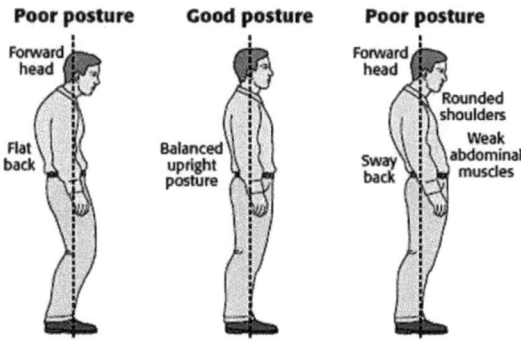

- **Walk:** Walk straight to have power in your chest and throw radiation through your waking style. This will give your personality a confident attitude.

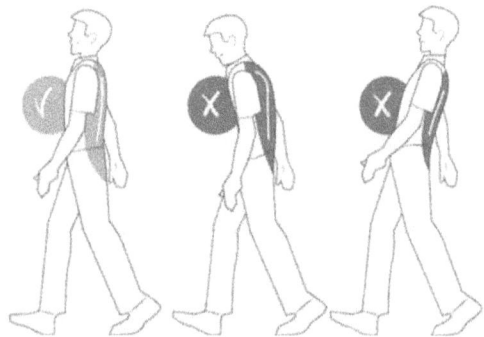

- **Hand Movements:** Open your hands whenever you speak to anyone new. Do not put your hands in your pockets. Initially, you will be worried about your hands; then, close your palms like this.

The raised steeple

The lowered steeple

- **Eye Contact:** Make eye contact with everyone to whom you speak. Make eye contact if you want to show confidence in others' minds. Remember the three-second rule? Don't stare at people.

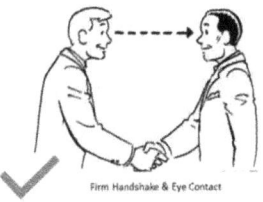

- **Sit:** When you sit, sit so you just have to enter the wrestling ring. See it this way. If possible, do not cross your legs. Keep them parallel.

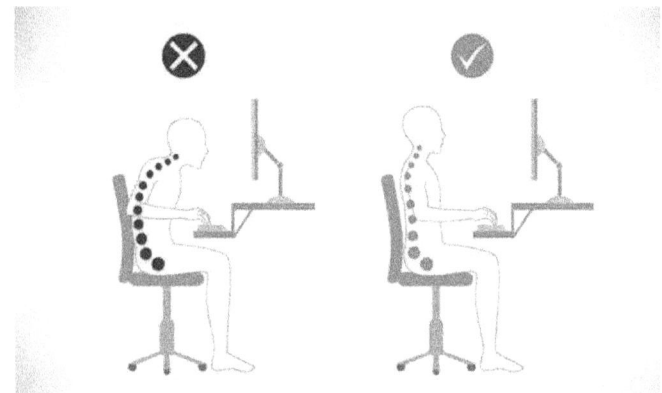

- **Speak:** Speak slowly and a little bit louder. People always perceive that a faster speaker is a good communicator, which is wrong. So, speak slowly and more audibly. It creates impact.

"Bhaiya, can you please explain the wrestling ring point? I didn't understand it. How is it to sit in a wrestling ring position?" I asked.

"Sure, a good point to catch, Mehul. I'm glad you're listening so attentively. When I say sit in a wrestling ring position, I mean that when a wrestler is waiting to go into the ring for a match, he will be sitting in a very attentive position. Like what I also call a cheetah position. He sits with his back straight, both legs parallel, and ready to move instead of being under the chair. When a wrestler comes in the ring, he doesn't come with shoulders down or walking slowly… he's fast, shoulders straight, chest bumping - to convey that he's ready to win. Similarly, when you meet new people, I'm not saying go jump and beat your chest - but walk with attitude, with confidence, so that the perception you give is positive."

"Hmm… Interesting, bhaiya," I replied, immediately correcting my slouching body and sitting more attentively. I thought about what Milind had spoken and suddenly asked, "Now I know why that dictionary salesman spoke with his hands. He was using his hand movements while talking to you. Did you observe, bhaiya?"

"Yes, Mehul, I did. Many companies train people in communication skills, such as speaking with people or collaborating with other companies. The salesman, Nivant Thakre's hand movements helped him communicate his message clearly and made him comfortable, probably reducing his fear of talking to strangers.

Your fear will be reduced when you use your body movements while speaking. All those strategies can be used whenever you meet new people or are in a public place so that they build an impression or create a perception of you in people's minds. You become used to these strategies by practising, which indirectly helps you grow."

"Very true, bhaiya. Now, I understand how to talk with people. I will use body language to my speaking style."

"Sure, Mehul. And I guarantee you will feel good about yourself. At first, you will feel conscious of what you are doing, but later, you will not even notice it, as it will come naturally to you. So, the crux of our communication discussion is that we should speak and behave in a way we want people to easily understand us and create the right perception in their mind."

"Listen Carefully, Mehul," continued Milind, "If you feel great inside, this should be reflected through your body language and speaking style. Most successful entrepreneurs and businessmen have not done any communications training, but they feel solid from the inside. Their mental state is so strong that it reflects on the outside."

"But what if I'm underconfident? What if I don't feel great from the inside?"

"Then you act confident. Use your body language to your advantage. No one will know if you're having butterflies in your stomach unless your body says it. Consciously work on your body language. Have you ever heard the phrase, fake it till you make it?"

"Yes, bhaiya," I smiled.

"Do it. Till you don't have to think about doing it, and it comes naturally to you. Whatever I am training or sharing with you is for the initial steps of the journey, which reaches the success stone. These tips are very helpful if you apply them in your career. Anyone who wants to go to the next level of communication can apply them."

"Wow, bhaiya. I never thought of such things in my life."

"I saw you change your sitting position earlier. From slouching, you became straighter and more attentive. That's a champion's body language. See Mehul, you can be comfortable with people you know. But communication creates impact and perception. Always remember this."

"Hmm…" is all I could muster.

"Yaar, I am hungry now. What's the time?" Milind suddenly asked.

I didn't realise how time flew away. I checked my watch; it was 1:24 PM.

"Bhaiya, I am also hungry now."

Today, I was not just hungry for food; I had a different kind of hunger: the hunger for growth, to achieve something in life. To start somewhere! I was highly motivated.

I left to wash my hands for lunch and started thinking how lucky I was. I was learning all this at this stage of life. Many people will be in business, service, or professional fields and want to grow and work with people. But if they learn about their strategies, their performance will change.

11

"Success leaves clues."

~ Tony Robbins

2:30 PM | Attitude (You See What You Are)

I went to the dining table for a lovely lunch of Akkha Masoor, Batata Bhajiya and Chapatis. As I was serving myself, I heard music. I looked up to see Milind had switched on the TV, and the song "Chale Chalo" was playing from the movie 'Lagaan.' This song was full of energy, motivation, leadership, teamwork, and a powerful call to action, or self-action, as bhaiya called it.

It was like divine intervention!

After the sumptuous lunch and freshening up, I returned to the training room to meet Milind for the next chapter. I was curious to know what would happen next.

"How was the lunch, Mehul?"

"Delicious, bhaiya, very fulfilling. Maushi is an excellent cook," I replied with a satisfied smile.

"So, you mean to say lunch was a success?" Milind asked.

"Umm, yeah, you can say so," I replied, confused as to why he was comparing lunch with success or failure.

Milind laughed at my struggle to comprehend, then said, "You see, Mehul, success is not always big. We often make it big in our minds. But it can be as small as the lunch you just enjoyed! Lunch was a success because it met your expectations and left you satisfied. The same principle applies to larger goals in life."

I began to see what he meant, though I couldn't fully comprehend it yet, so I nodded.

"Just imagine," Milind continued, "There are regular successes and failures in all we do, whether small or big. Let me tell you this—our attitude towards these outcomes defines the course of everything. If you approach every situation with the mindset that you can learn something valuable, even failures become stepping stones."

I leaned forward, intrigued. "So, it's all about how we see things?"

"Exactly," Milind said. "Success and failure are just outcomes. What truly defines them is our perception, how we see it. A businessman may view a failed business as a learning experience and move on to the next venture. But for another individual, it may seem like the end of the road. How you perceive things - whether your mindset is positive or negative - will determine whether you give up or try again, especially with your new learning experience.

Milind paused, letting his words sink in. "Remember, what's gone is gone. The restart attitude I mentioned earlier is important. Focus on the future and what you can achieve next, rather than living in your past failures."

It felt like I was witnessing a change in my attitude. "So, it's about continuous learning and moving forward?"

"Yes," he confirmed. "In life, you will have to deal with many problems and challenges. If you develop a positive attitude and see each experience as a growth opportunity, you can handle success and failure better. Like lunch, enjoy the successes, learn from the failures, and keep moving on."

"But how do we feel happy in failures, bhaiya?" I asked.

"You see, Mehul, in a framework, what impacts our behaviour is how we think, feel, or behave in a situation. People see our behaviour or reaction but do not know what is happening inside us—how we think and believe or why we behave the way we do.

What we think and feel depends on the areas in which we have involved ourselves and the experiences we have gained. For example, reading different kinds of books, watching diverse videos, meeting new people, and facing various challenges all contribute to shaping our mindset.

From age 21 to 29, one should gain new experiences, meet all kinds of people, visit new places, collaborate with different people, accept new challenges, and even face new failures—this will open one's mind and change one's thinking and feelings.

Small failures will not hamper you if you've taken on many life challenges because you have built that thick muscle. These things help us shape our attitudes.

Imagine an individual who has not done much in life; his thought process will likely be rigid and unchanging. He will not divert from it because he doesn't know any better. On the other hand, if parents intentionally involve their children in some out-of-the-box or uncomfortable situations, like guided mentorship, they can face more challenges and new situations as they grow up. They gain confidence and have a settled way of thinking—that is what I call an attitude," Milind concluded.

Feeling inspired, I thanked him. I realised this new chapter was about developing a growth mindset and looking at life through continuous improvement and persistence.

12

"Until you value yourself, you will not value your time. Until you value your time, you will not do anything with it."

~ M. Scott Peck

4:00 PM | Time Management

After we discussed attitude and mindset, Milind and I settled into our seats with cups of tea. He had a knack for making complex ideas relatable, and I was eager to learn more from him.

"Mehul, have you ever heard the saying 'Time is money'?" Milind asked, taking a sip of his tea.

"Of course, bhaiya. It's quite a common phrase," I replied.

Milind smiled. "Well, I disagree with that saying. I believe time is much more than money."

"How?" I leaned in, curious to learn more.

"Imagine if I offered you 5 crore rupees and asked you to take me back to 15 August 1947. Could you do it for 5 crores or even 50?"

I thought for a moment and shook my head. "No, of course not. Time travel isn't possible, and no amount of money can bring back the past."

"Exactly," Milind said. "The time that has passed is gone forever. You can earn back lost money but can't reclaim lost time. This is why time is far more valuable than money."

I nodded slowly, starting to understand his point.

"But bhaiya, what if someone invented the time machine in the future? It may be a possibility," I asked.

"Let's work with what we have in the present. Let's not think about a hypothetical future," Milind said sternly. "Now, here's another thing to consider: people often say they don't have enough time. We all get the same 24 hours daily, don't we? Or does someone get 25 or 26 hours?"

"Of course, bhaiya, everyone gets the same amount of time in a day," I replied.

"Then, it's not about having enough time; it's about prioritising your time and having the right focus. The results depend on what and where we focus our efforts," Milind concluded.

"That makes sense," I said. "So, if someone says they don't have time, does that mean they're focusing on the wrong activities?"

"Exactly," Milind said. "They're not concentrating on what's truly important to them. So, the question arises: where should we focus?"

Milind paused for a moment, letting me think about this.

"This brings us to the Pareto Principle," he continued. "According to this principle, only 20% of our tasks give

80% of results. The key is to identify and focus on those 20% tasks."

"Can you explain this a bit more?" I asked.

"Sure," Milind said. "Imagine a professional working in a company. They might work extremely hard daily, but hard work alone doesn't guarantee a promotion. However, suppose they analyse their tasks, identify the ones that significantly impact the company's bottom line—their 20%—and focus on those. In that case, they are much more likely to get noticed and appreciated. This could lead to a promotion."

"Hmm..." I said thoughtfully. "So, the focus should be on tasks that create the most value."

"Exactly," Milind said. "Clarity and focus on the right tasks can make a huge difference. It's about working smarter, not just harder."

"Now, how do I choose which task to focus on?" I asked.

"Let me give you an example," continued Milind. "Every individual has a per-hour cost. For example, a newly graduated guy gets a job worth 30,000 rupees. So, his per-hour cost is about 250 rupees. What he needs to do now is shift his focus to tasks, skills, and crafts so that his per-hour cost increases. He should only be involved in those activities."

"Hmm," I said in a deep thought.

"If you chat with your friends, does your per-hour cost increase? No." Milind continued without waiting for my answer, "But if the chat helps refresh your mind, you should chat with your friends. Or if a book helps you grow, increases your knowledge, and ultimately increases your per-hour cost, you must read it."

"So, how do we use our time in the best possible way?" I asked.

"Given the Pareto principle, only 20% of tasks give 80% results. We should work in cycles. The human mind works in low-focus and high-focus cycles. For example, if you work on something high-focus for an hour and then take a break and work on something low-focus, your mind will freshen up."

"Can you give me an example?" I asked.

"Sure," Milind said. "Say you've been writing a book and focusing on it for an hour or more. Then, immediately do something low-focus, like cleaning your desk or listening to music, to freshen up your mind and recharge."

"Another example," Milind continued, "High-Focus: Exercising. Low Focus: Music. You will see that in the gym, people usually listen to music in the background when focusing on their exercises."

"That's true," I said. "So, if we use these combinations, our mind remains fresh, we can work longer, and we don't get bored."

"Exactly," Milind said.

"What about deciding the priority of tasks?" I asked

"If you're confused about the task's priority, you should again decide based on the per-hour cost. The first question I ask myself when taking on a new task or meeting a new client is: Is it increasing my value? If the answer is yes, then I will do the task or meet the person."

"I got it," I said. "The key is ensuring our tasks align with our long-term goals and focusing on activities that increase our value."

"Exactly," Milind said. Time management is about making conscious choices with your focus. Use these strategies to improve your productivity and overall satisfaction significantly."

Milind took another sip of tea and continued, "Apart from focusing on the right tasks, it's also crucial to understand the difference between doing the correct thing and correcting things. Tell me, Mehul, if Ratan Tata decides to clean his garden, he might do a great job. But is that the best use of his time?"

"Probably not," I said, smiling.

"Right," Milind agreed. "During the time he spends cleaning his garden, he could make decisions that have a far greater impact on his business. It's about utilising your time based on your roles and goals."

"So, it's not just about time management but also about prioritising the right work," I thought loudly. I felt a sense of clarity as Milind spoke. His practical approach to time management was starting to make a lot of sense.

"Bhaiya, how can I apply this in my own life?" I asked.

"Start by analysing your daily tasks," Milind suggested. "Identify which ones have the most significant impact on your goals. Focus on those tasks and minimise time spent on less important activities. This will help you maximise your productivity."

"That sounds doable," I said.

"Also," Milind added, "remember to avoid the trap of perfectionism. Sometimes, we spend too much time perfecting minor details instead of focusing on the bigger picture. It's better to do the right thing well enough than to waste time trying to make everything perfect."

"How can I avoid that?" I asked.

"Set clear goals and deadlines for each task," Milind advised. "Focus on completing the task within the given time frame rather than making it perfect. Review your work, learn from mistakes, and improve in the next attempt. This way, you keep moving forward and avoid getting stuck."

"I can see how that would save a lot of time," I said thoughtfully.

"And finally," Milind concluded, "embrace the 'restart' attitude we discussed earlier. Don't dwell on past mistakes or lost time. Focus on the present and future, and keep moving forward."

Our conversation had given me a lot to think about. I realised that my approach to time management needed an overhaul. It wasn't just about being busy but being productive and focusing on what truly mattered.

As I finished my tea, I thanked Milind for his valuable insights. "Bhaiya, you've given me a new perspective on time management. I feel more equipped to handle my tasks and priorities now."

"I'm glad to hear that, Mehul," Milind said warmly. "Remember, time is precious. Use it wisely, and always focus on what truly matters. And that reminds me, what's the time?"

"My God, it's almost 7.00 PM, bhaiya. I didn't even realise where the time went," I said, looking at my watch.

"Well, let's call it a day then, Mehul," Milind said.

"Yes, bhaiya," I agreed.

After this long but fruitful day, we had an early dinner of Pav Bhaji, and I went to my room. With this newfound knowledge, I felt inspired and ready to apply these principles in my life. Milind's practical advice on time management enlightened me and motivated me to make the most of every moment.

Day - 3

13

"We learn our belief systems as very little children, and then we move through life creating experiences to match our beliefs."

~ Louise Hay

5:45 AM | Belief

After a peaceful night's sleep, I woke up at 5 AM, quickly freshened up, and went downstairs to meet Milind in the garden outside. I guess I was early as Milind hadn't come yet.

I brought my diary and pen to start my first day of morning rituals. I began by writing about all I had learnt yesterday and how I wanted to divide my upcoming days. I saw Milind coming out in the garden, and we exchanged our morning greetings. For the next 20 minutes, we went to the society park and did some brisk walking and light exercises. I was already feeling refreshed when we returned to his house and started meditating.

This 20:20:20 ritual was healthy for my body and my spirit. I felt relaxed and ready to face the world.

It was 6:30 AM, and the sun was just beginning to rise, casting a soft golden hue across the sky. The early morning stillness was the perfect backdrop for our following conversation.

"Mehul," Milind began, "let's discuss something very important today—the belief system."

I nodded, intrigued. "Sure, bhaiya."

"In my training sessions," Milind continued, "I tell a story about creating a belief."

"Please share the story with me too, bhaiya," I requested.

"Have you heard about the story of Abhimanyu from Mahabharata?" Milind asked.

"Arjun's son? The one who died while getting in the '*chakravyuh*'?" I said.

"Yes, but he did not die while getting in the *chakravyuh*. He was killed because he did not know how to get out of it. Do you know why?"

"Umm… he did not learn it?!?"

"No, he did not. He was still in his mother's womb when Arjun narrated the strategy to Subhadra, Abhimanyu's mother. She slept while listening to the story," Milind informed, "so she couldn't hear the second part, the strategy of getting out of the *chakravyuh* part, and therefore, neither could he."

"Really?" I asked.

"Did you know that this is scientifically proven and is believed by doctors today, that if a woman has a child in her womb, the happiness and positive environment she creates in the house will impact the child accordingly?"

My eyes widened with curiosity. "Really, bhaiya? How does that work?"

"Imagine," Milind explained, "a ball of clay is there instead of the child's brain. If you press the clay ball with a finger, it will leave an impression there. Similarly, the child's belief system is created right from when they are in their mother's womb. When they are born, their first contact is with their parents. From there, they learn what crying or laughing is."

"That's fascinating," I said thoughtfully. "So, our environment shapes us even before we are born."

"Exactly," Milind agreed. "Every individual absorbs some attributes from their parents—like how they laugh, walk, and talk. Call it DNA or simply copying, but an impressionable child would've unknowingly copied their parents. Crying comes naturally to children, but they absorb the rest from their surroundings. Then, they come in contact with the extended family—grandparents, uncles, aunts, cousins, and then school—teachers and peers. What I'm trying to say is that your thought process depends on how and where you have been brought up. Your belief system depends on your upbringing, whether in a business or service-class family."

I nodded, understanding the deep impact of one's environment on shaping beliefs. "So, basically, our experiences and surroundings mould our mindset."

"Yes, exactly," Milind said. "I also read somewhere that if we, as individuals, have an aptitude for learning, we can change our belief system at any time. When our thought process converts into a pattern, it is called a mindset. For example, 'This is who I am or how I am.' It is set in my mind, like, 'This always happens to me.' Or, 'Even if I do a lot of hard work, I don't get rewarded accordingly'—this belief system I have created in my mind."

"That makes sense," I said. "So, you're saying what we achieve depends on our belief system. Whether we can do it or think we can't, depends on how we believe."

"Exactly, Mehul," Milind replied with a smile. "Our belief system is like the foundation of a building. If it's strong and positive, it can support great achievements. But if it's weak and negative, it can crumble under pressure."

Milind paused momentarily, then continued, "It's like the story I tell in my training. Imagine a child growing up in a home filled with love and encouragement. The parents always tell the child, 'You can achieve anything you set your mind to.' This child grows up believing in their potential and confidently takes on challenges. And then there's another child in a different home where the parents are always critical, saying things like, 'You're not good enough,' or 'You'll never succeed.' This child grows up with self-doubt and fear of failure."

"It's sad to think how much negative beliefs can hold someone back," I said, shaking my head.

"It is," Milind agreed. "But the good news is, we can change our belief systems. It's not easy, but it's possible. It starts with awareness—recognising our negative beliefs and challenging them. This pattern empowers people."

"How do we do that?" I asked eagerly.

"Well, we can correct the child by giving assertive feedback, such as what he did well and what he can do differently," Milind said. "First, we need to identify the negative beliefs. Write them down. For example, if you believe, 'I'm not good at public speaking,' write it down. Then, challenge it. Ask yourself, 'Is this true? What evidence do I have to support this belief? What evidence do I have that contradicts it?' Often, you'll find that these beliefs are not based on facts but on past experiences or things people have told you."

"That sounds like a powerful exercise," I remarked.

"It is," Milind nodded. "And once you've challenged the negative beliefs, replace them with positive ones. Instead of saying, 'I'm not good at public speaking,' say, 'I'm improving at public speaking every day.' Practice affirmations and visualise yourself succeeding. Over time, these new positive beliefs will become your new mindset."

I leaned back, processing everything bhaiya had shared. "This is really insightful, bhaiya. It makes me think about my beliefs and how they might hold me back."

Milind smiled warmly. "That's the first step, Mehul. Awareness. Once you're aware, you can start making changes. Remember, our beliefs shape our reality. If we believe we can achieve something, we're more likely to take the necessary actions. But if we believe we can't, we've already defeated ourselves before we even start."

"True," I said thoughtfully. "I guess it's all about having a growth mindset and being open to learning and changing."

"Exactly," Milind said. "A growth mindset is important. It's about believing that our abilities and intelligence can be developed with effort, learning, and persistence. It's about seeing challenges as opportunities to grow rather than obstacles to overcome."

I smiled, feeling inspired. "Thank you, bhaiya. This talk has opened my eyes. I'm going to start working on my beliefs and mindset."

Bhaiya patted me on the back. "I'm glad to hear that, Mehul. Remember, it's a journey. Be patient with yourself and keep moving forward. You have the power to shape your destiny with your beliefs."

"Let's go, get freshened up, and see you at breakfast," Milind said as we both got up.

14

*"We are what we repeatedly do.
Excellence, then, is not an act but a habit."*

~ Will Durant

8:15 AM | Habit Formation and Procrastination

I reached the breakfast table and saw that Bhaiya was waiting for me. The table was already laid, and today, we had *Farali Thalipeeth* for breakfast, another speciality from the Maharashtrian cuisine. The pancake made of sabudana and potatoes was delicious and very filling.

While having breakfast, bhaiya told me he was happy to see me start practising my morning rituals.

"This is how you will form a habit," Milind said.

"How long does it take to form a habit, bhaiya?" I asked.

"Consistency is the key, Mehul," Milind replied.

"I've been struggling with keeping up my habits lately. What if I miss my morning rituals, bhaiya?"

"Well, when I talk about consistency," Milind explained, "people usually think it means being regular all the time. But I've come to understand consistency is how quickly we return to our routine after a break. Let me give you an example."

I nodded, listening intently.

"I've been going to the gym regularly for the last eight years," Milind continued. "Now, if I miss going to the gym for four days, I could feel guilty by the fifth day. This guilt might linger for a couple of days, and then for the next 5-6 days, I'd be stuck thinking, 'Damn, I missed the gym.' If I don't go for five days and then spend the next few days just feeling guilty, I've lost ten days of gym time. The key is to restart on the fifth day without overthinking, just like I'm in machine mode."

"That makes sense. So, you're saying it's about how quickly we bounce back, not just about never missing a day," I smiled understandingly.

"Exactly," Milind said, smiling. "I follow two golden rules:

1: Just do it.

2: If there's a break, restart and do it again.

When you work this way, you won't feel bad or guilty for missing a few days and won't be angry at yourself for taking a break. This can apply to any habit—going to the gym, reading, or any other good habit. Just stop overthinking about the break and restart."

"That's such a relief to hear," Mehul admitted. "I always beat myself up when I miss a few days of my routine."

Milind nodded. "Most of us do, but it's counterproductive. Another thing I've found helpful is adjusting the time. For instance, if I lack time and can't do my regular one-hour workout, I'll take 10-15 minutes to exercise instead. This way, my brain gets the message that I've done some workout. Even if I'm unwell, I'll do light exercises like walking. This prevents guilt and gives me peace of mind."

"So, it's about flexibility and keeping the momentum going, even if it's just a little bit," I concluded.

"Exactly," Milind said. "It's okay to take a break between your habits or routine. The problem emerges when you don't restart immediately after the break. To form a habit or routine, take small steps. Set small, achievable goals and then increase the target slowly and steadily."

I nodded, listening intently, making notes.

"Start Small"

"What do you mean by this, bhaiya?"

"Make smaller goals. For example, if someone wants to read a book but lacks time or motivation, I tell them to set a target of 10 minutes every day. Keep the book where it is easily accessible, like your bedside table. Read for 10 minutes before you fall asleep or during breaks at work. Maybe you read one page a day or ten, but do it every day."

"Small, consistent actions build up over time," I said, nodding. "It's manageable and less intimidating."

"Exactly," Milind agreed. "The concept of habit formation is about creating a system that works for you. It's not about being perfect 365 days a year. Humans are bound to face distractions—travel, festivities, health issues. Consistency isn't about never breaking the routine but how quickly we recover from those breaks."

I leaned back on the sofa, reflecting on Milind's words. "This is helpful, bhaiya. I've always thought of consistency as an all-or-nothing approach, and when I failed, I felt like giving up."

"I used to think that way too," Milind admitted. "But once I started seeing consistency as the speed of recovery, everything changed. It became more sustainable and less stressful."

"That's a game-changer," I said, excited and smiling. "I'm going to start applying these principles to my routines."

Milind patted me on the back. "I'm glad to hear that. Remember, it's a journey. Be patient with yourself and keep moving forward. Small steps, taken consistently, lead to big changes over time."

As we sat together, enjoying our coffee, the conversation shifted to our personal experiences with habits and routines. Milind shared how he had applied these principles in various aspects of his life, from fitness to learning new skills.

"I remember when I first started learning to play the guitar," Milind said. "I was so excited but overwhelmed by how much there was to learn. I decided to apply the same principles of habit formation. I started with just 10 minutes of practice each day. Gradually, as I became more comfortable, I increased the time. It's a regular part of my day, and I've made significant progress."

"That's inspiring," I said. "I've always wanted to learn a new language but felt daunted by the commitment. Maybe I should start with just a few minutes each day."

"Absolutely," Milind encouraged. "The key is to start small and build up gradually. Consistency in small doses is more effective than sporadic bursts of effort."

I nodded, feeling motivated. "I'm going to give it a try. Starting today, I'll spend 10 minutes each morning learning French. I'll keep my materials on my desk to remind me."

"That's a great plan," Milind said. "Remember, don't beat yourself up if you miss a day. Just get back to it the next day. That's the real essence of consistency."

I started planning to follow my routine when I heard bhaiya saying to take a break and meet for lunch.

15

"A strong, positive self-image is the best possible preparation for success."

~ Joyce Brothers

1:30 | Personality Development

Dahi Samosa vs Saada Samosa

I freshened up in my room and reached the dining table. I saw the table laid, but Milind was not around. Maushi had served Samosa for lunch. Samosa for lunch! I wondered. It's a snack we usually eat during tea time. However, I wasn't very hungry, as the breakfast was heavy. So, I picked up the newspaper on the coffee table while waiting for Milind to join me.

He came from his office/training room and informed me that there were some urgent emails that he needed to reply to. I just nodded, but internally, I was impressed by his work style and organisational skills. He divided his time and was very well-organised. I realised that a leader becomes a leader not just by what he says but more so by what he does. His actions were more inspirational than what he said.

I was about to serve myself when bhaiya stopped me.

"Today, let me serve you," Milind said while picking up a plate.

He picked up two Samosas, put them on a plate, and put the plate on the table in the centre.

He picked up another plate and layered it with some boiled chickpeas. He then picked up two samosas and crushed them a little with his hands, putting them on top of the chickpeas on the plate. Then he poured some beaten *dahi*, which had already been mixed with salt, sugar, and a little pepper, on top of the samosas. He added red and green chutneys. He finished it by garnishing it with some *sev, anar* and *dhaniya*.

He then put this plate next to the plain samosa plate and asked me to pick one.

"Umm..." I hesitated.

"Don't be shy. Just pick the one you want to eat," encouraged Milind.

I sheepishly picked the Dahi Samosa and let the plain samosa plate remain on the table.

"Well done, Mehul," Milind said. "Now tell me, why did you pick the Dahi Samosa and not the plain one? They both are, ultimately, Samosas."

"Umm... it looked tastier, more inviting," I replied honestly.

"Mehul, before today, did you ever think about the difference between a plain samosa and a dahi samosa?" he asked, grinning like a kid about to share a secret.

I smiled back and replied, "Not really, bhaiya. I mean, I always thought samosas are samosas, right?"

He shook his head, still smiling. "Think about it. A plain samosa, or Saada Samosa, is just as tasty and well-made. But when you add dahi and chutneys and garnish them with sev and pomegranate seeds, it looks far more appealing. People are drawn to it."

I started to see his point. "So, the samosa developed a personality when it became dahi samosa?"

"Exactly!" Milind exclaims. "A Saada Samosa is like a basic personality. It has depth but doesn't attract attention if not presented well. On the other hand, a Dahi Samosa is a developed, charismatic personality. It's the same core but presented in a way that attracts or invites people."

He picked up the plain samosa plate and repeated the process of turning it into dahi samosa. We chatted about my father's restaurant, and I told Milind I would suggest he add dahi samosas to his menu along with plain samosas. Milind laughed.

"People often say, 'We are what we are. Why should we change?'" Milind continued. "But we don't achieve success just like that. We attract success by becoming the person who draws it in."

He took a bite of his dahi samosa and gestured for emphasis. "Take, for instance, a successful doctor. He doesn't start earning well from day 1 of practice. He spent years studying, getting certified, and gaining experience. He's a doctor because of his hard work and perseverance, not because he charges high fees."

I nodded, understanding his point. "So, it's about the journey and the effort, not just the result."

"Precisely," Milind said, smiling. "People want success but don't want to go through the long, hard, and often boring process to get there. They want to learn to swim but fear jumping into the water. True personality development requires consistent effort, even when it's tedious. It's about doing the same task repeatedly until you master it, following routines without fail."

As we continued eating, I realised how much sense Milind was making. "So, when people ask why they need to look presentable, it's not just about appearances?" I asked curiously.

"Absolutely," Milind replied. "It's about creating a perception. Remember, I told you yesterday that we live in a perception-driven world? When you meet someone new, you're judged based on your appearance before speaking. It's not about wearing expensive clothes or brands, but about presenting yourself in a way that suits your personality and the situation."

He paused to let that sink in before continuing. "And notice how your confidence rises when you're dressed well. When starting your career, you must be mindful of how you present yourself. Eventually, as you succeed, people will look beyond your clothes and see your work and accomplishments."

I nodded as I thought about what Milind had just said.

"Like how we know our president, Dr. APJ Abdul Kalam for his work, not his hairstyle, or remember Gandhi for his impact, not the way he dressed."

"Exactly," Milind says. "Initially, you need to become the dahi samosa to get noticed. But once people recognise you for your work, those superficial aspects become secondary."

We finished our samosas and moved to the other room. I felt like I'd gained more than just a satisfying meal. Milind had given me a fresh perspective on personality development.

"Bhaiya," I asked, "why do people resist changing themselves to be more presentable? They always say, 'I am what I am.'"

Milind nodded thoughtfully. "It's because they misunderstand the concept of authenticity. Being authentic doesn't mean you never change or improve. It means staying true to your core values and principles while continuously working to become the best version of yourself."

Milind leaned back in his chair, looking out the window. "Imagine if a doctor thought, 'I am what I am, so I don't need further training or certification.' Would you trust that doctor? Of course not. The same goes for personal development. You need to grow and adapt while staying true to yourself."

I reflected on this, realising how important it is to balance authenticity and growth. "So, it's about evolving while staying grounded in your core values."

"Exactly," Milind said. "And that's the key to attracting success. You become a person who naturally draws people in, not by changing who you are fundamentally, but by enhancing and presenting yourself in the best possible light."

Our lunch conversation made me think deeply about my journey ahead. I realised I've often shied away from certain opportunities because I wasn't confident enough. But now, I have started to see that confidence comes from preparation and presentation, and I promised myself to be more confident in developing my personality.

16

"Champions are not the ones who always win races - champions are the ones who get out there and try. And try harder the next time."

~ Simon Sinek

4 PM | Secrets of Champions

After lunch, Milind and I took a break from our lessons and met again around 4 PM for the next session.

Milind got a coffee and looked at me, "Mehul, why are you looking disappointed? What happened?"

I looked up, surprised that he had noticed it.

"Don't look surprised. You just told me without saying a word. Your face is not the usual enthusiastic self. Your body is slumping, and you seem distracted. Is everything alright with you?" Milind said.

I nodded, "Bhaiya, I just got a call from one of the companies I interviewed with. I got rejected."

"Hmm…" was all Milind said.

"I answered every question correctly, but I was nervous, and I stammered a bit. I always get nervous in an interview or when talking to a stranger," I continued, feeling upset.

"Are you a champion, Mehul?" Milind asked.

"What?" I replied, confused.

"A champion is a person who remains undefeated. Do you want to become a champion?" Milind rephrased his question.

"Of course I do," I replied.

"Then let me share a secret with you, Mehul. What makes champions truly unbeatable?" Milind asked.

"What?" I asked.

"You can't defeat someone who doesn't care about pain, failure, rejection, loss, disrespect, or heartbreak."

I was intrigued. "That's quite a statement, bhaiya. Can you please explain more?" I asked as I poured a cup for myself.

"Sure," Milind replied. "Think about it. Champions have this unique trait of not letting success or failure get to their heads. They don't take anything personally. They enjoy life but stay grounded. Whether they succeed or fail, they keep moving forward because, for them, progress is happiness."

I listened carefully.

Milind continued, "When I ask my students – how many of them used to take their class 10th or 12th seriously – because their parents told them that the class X or XII results would make or break them. Most of them would raise their hands. And then I ask them, when they look back, how many can now laugh at their younger self? Most of them agree again. It now seems so trivial when looking back. However, I tell them it used to feel huge and permanent back then. But people realise as they grow, things change; they are temporary.

Similarly, today's problems or difficulties may seem permanent, but they are not. Therefore, real happiness is in progress. What you have achieved is good; instead of celebrating it forever, move and look for the next celebration—that is actual happiness."

"Interesting," I mused. "So, it's all about their mindset?"

Milind nodded. "Exactly. Let me break it down for you. I have a few points that I always tell my students about the secret of success. Now, it's up to them whether they want to include them in their lives or not."

I leaned forward, took out my diary and pen, and started to note the points Milind was about to make.

"You leaned forward, which means your body language is telling me that you are interested in what we are about to discuss," Milind noticed.

"Of course, bhaiya, I'm very interested," I smiled. "Please continue."

"Okay, the starting point I always say is that '**Champions are Selfish**' in a positive way. Why, you may ask?"

I nodded.

"They work on themselves because they have high expectations and value personal growth. They demand more from themselves because they want to add value to everything they do," Milind replied.

I said, "That makes sense. If you don't expect much from yourself, you won't push yourself to achieve more."

"Right," Milind continued. "Then we come to '**The Right Mindset**'. Champions understand that life is 80% psychology and 20% mechanics. It's all in the mind. They read books, surround themselves with like-minded people, and take courses to train their minds. They know that a strong mindset is crucial."

"Training the mind, huh?" I said thoughtfully. "Yesterday, you said it's all about how you think and perceive things."

"Exactly, that's how you train your mind." Milind agreed. "Next is the '**Power of Now**'. Champions believe in action. Ideas are great, but without action, they're meaningless. They focus on implementing their ideas rather than just thinking about them."

I nodded in agreement. "I've seen so many people with great ideas who never take the steps to bring them to life, especially in our small towns."

Milind smiled. "That's why champions stand out. They act. '**The Principle of Give and Take**' - now, this is crucial. Champions understand that to achieve anything in life, they must add value to others first. The rule is about giving before you take. If you help people achieve what they want, they will help you achieve what you want."

"That's a great principle," I said. "It's like creating a positive cycle of giving and receiving."

"Exactly," Milind said. "To become a champion, one must be '**Solution-Oriented**.' Champions don't dwell on problems; they focus on solutions. They immediately shift their mindset to 'What's next?' or 'What can we do best in this situation?'"

I raised my coffee cup in agreement. "That's a powerful approach. It keeps you moving forward rather than getting stuck."

Milind continued, "Let's now talk about '**Expertise**.' To be a champion, you must be an expert in at least one skill or craft. You can master a few others, but being an expert in one area is key."

"That's so true," I said. "You need to have that one thing you excel at."

"Absolutely," Milind said. "As we discussed earlier, '**keep moving, whether it's success or failure**.' Champions believe in progress. They don't live in the past; they always look forward to the next challenge."

I leaned back, wondering. "It's like not letting setbacks or failures define you."

"Exactly, or even let success get to your head," Milind said. "Now we come to '**Competing with Oneself**'. Champions don't compare themselves with others. They focus on their own progress. It's about being better than you were yesterday."

"Comparison can be so damaging," I agreed. "It can really break your spirit."

Milind nodded. "That's why champions compete with themselves. They use their progress as a benchmark. Champions are also driven by a purpose, '**Hunger and Stubbornness**'. They are always hungry for growth and development and are stubborn in their pursuit of success.

They take risks because they are never satisfied with where they are."

"That's the spirit of a true champion," I said admiringly. "Always pushing the boundaries."

"Exactly," Milind said. "They also should have an '**Iron Flame Spirit**.' Champions don't let the flame of their dreams die. They protect and continuously work on it, no matter what external factors come their way."

I smiled. "That's inspiring. Keeping the dream alive no matter what."

"Finally," Milind concluded, "it is all about '**Being Imperfectly Perfect**.' Champions know that perfection is a myth. They don't aim for perfection; they aim for progress. They believe in doing things and improving along the way."

I nodded vigorously. "Perfection can be paralysing. It's better to keep moving and improving."

Milind leaned back, satisfied with the conversation. "Exactly, Mehul. These are the secrets of champions. They focus on progress, mindset, action, giving value, solutions, expertise, personal competition, hunger, resilience, and understanding that perfection is a myth. They are always evolving, always moving forward."

I stopped taking notes and said, "You know, bhaiya, I think I've been holding back because I was afraid of failure and rejection, especially because of the stammer in my speech. But now, I see that those are just part of the journey. It's about how you respond to the failure and rejection that matters."

Milind smiled warmly. "That's the spirit, Mehul. What I have noticed is you stammer only when you're nervous. You did initially when you came, but now look at you!"

I smiled.

"Embrace the journey, focus on your growth, and keep moving forward. That's the true essence of being a champion," Milind said.

As we finished our coffee and conversations, I felt a renewed sense of determination. The conversation gave me a fresh perspective on success and what it truly means to be a champion. I realised it wasn't about avoiding failure or rejection but embracing them as part of the journey and continuously striving to improve.

Milind's insights sparked a fire in me, and I was ready to take on new challenges with a champion's mindset.

"It's still early, so let's get an ice cream, shall we?" Milind asked me.

"Sure, bhaiya. But this time, I'm treating you," I replied.

"Why not?" Milind laughed, and we went for an evening stroll to refresh our bodies, souls, and, of course, our taste buds!

17

"Brand yourself for the career you want, not the job you have."

~ Dan Schawbel

7.00 PM | Brand in You

It was the end of a long weekend, three days of life-altering training. Milind and I, however, were still in deep conversation as we walked back home after having the ice cream. We had been discussing various topics throughout the last three days, and now it was time to wrap up. Tonight, dinner consisted of Bharli Bhendi, Masala Bhat, and chapatis. Maushi, I smiled, was making sure I enjoyed Marathi cuisine during my trip. It was simple yet delicious food.

As we served the food on our plates, Milind started the conversation. He told me he had recently read a book on personal branding that resonated deeply with him and was eager to share its insights with me.

"Mehul," Milind began, leaning back in his chair. "This is the 21st century, and we're already in 2005. You must have read about the last big revolution in your history books - the Industrial Revolution. How have things changed since then? Now, we're at the beginning of what we call a digital revolution."

"True, bhaiya. So many things have changed since the internet connected us all," Mehul said.

"Yes," Milind continued. "The Internet is impacting our lives faster than we know. There will soon be a time when everything will become "online." We are now dependent on Google for our research. People abroad have started using the internet for "shopping" online. All they need to do is click on the product, which will be delivered to your doorstep. And I'm sure this will soon come to India as well. Can you imagine! You don't go out to buy things; they come to your home, and you pay up. Very soon, there will come a time when people will even get their news online, maybe even work from home or anywhere. They will just have to connect to the internet."

"Wow, bhaiya! Can this happen in our lifetime?" I was excited at the prospect.

"Why not? The world is changing so fast with digital innovations every day. You have a cell phone - could you imagine carrying a phone with you at all times just 10 years ago?" *Nahi, na…* so imagine what may evolve in another 10 years!"

"You're right, bhaiya," I agreed.

"But you know, there's something very important that we should not forget," Milind said.

I took a bite of my food, and curiously, I asked. "What is it, bhaiya?"

Milind smiled. "I've taught you about personality development and communication skills. How you project yourself to others is extremely important in succeeding in life. You should be very careful about how you communicate verbally and with your body language."

"Yes, bhaiya." Mehul nodded.

"That unique personality that you create will be your brand. However, before artificially building a brand by projecting an image to others, we should focus on our inner brand. The inner brand is what truly lasts."

I nodded, trying to grasp what Milind was getting at.

"What I'm trying to say is that," Milind simplified, "instead of focusing on creating an artificial image, we should concentrate on developing an authentic and internal personality. This means building a unique personal brand based on who we truly are. Just like famous brands are known for their distinct qualities, our personalities should reflect our unique characteristics. If we stay true to ourselves, our personal brand will naturally attract others and leave a lasting impression. And that is the mantra of success."

I nodded. "So, you're saying the focus should be inside first, then outside?"

"Exactly," Milind said. "It should be an inside-outside approach. Build yourself from the inside first, and let that naturally reflect on the outside. This way, when you build your brand inside, you become authentically YOU. That's why the concept is called BI-YOU - the Brand In You."

"Interesting concept," I remarked. "But how do we start building this inner brand?"

Milind leaned forward, his eyes bright with enthusiasm. "It begins with understanding that we are unique. Some people may look like us but don't think, feel, or behave like us. We're unmatchable, so there's no point in trying to become someone else. Everything starts with you."

I smiled. "True. So, what are the key steps to building this inner brand?"

Milind listed them on his fingers. "First, accept yourself. The more you accept yourself, the more powerful and learnable you become. Second, if you can't help yourself, you can't help others. Third, your growth depends on your mindset. Fourth, not taking action is more dangerous than being positively distracted."

I started scribbling notes furiously. "These are great points, bhaiya. What else?"

Milind continued, "Reflection is the best way to learn. Success is 5% strategy and 95% consistency. Remember, not everyone is for you, and you are not for everyone. It's okay to identify your way of having fun. Money is necessary, so understand it and learn to handle it. Miracles happen when you're true to yourself."

I nodded, taking in the shared wisdom. "So, it's about being consistent, reflective, and true to oneself."

"Exactly," Milind agreed. "And there's more. You either do it or don't; there's no trying. If you're brutally honest with yourself, you don't need anyone else to decide. Discipline matters more than talent. People will only see your actions, not your intentions."

I smiled. "That's a tough one. We often want people to understand our intentions."

"True," Milind said, "but actions speak louder. Also, there's a difference between earning, managing, and investing money. Blaming is the fastest way to degrade yourself. You're more powerful than you think if you're comfortable with yourself. And remember, perfect people only exist in pictures hanging on a wall - with garland on them."

I was shocked. "That's a sad and gloomy way to put it, but it's still accurate."

Milind grinned. "It's true. You have to work very hard at least once in your life. It could be in childhood, adulthood, middle age, or old age - the choice is yours. And there will be a time when you'll feel utterly useless and think the world is against you. But once you overcome that, you'll be unstoppable."

I was silent for a moment and then said, "It's about building a strong inner personality that can adapt to different roles and challenges, right?"

"Yes," Milind said. "The stronger your core, your inner self, the easier it is to transition into various roles, whether at work, at home, or anywhere else. It's about building a foundation that is strong yet flexible."

I smiled. "That makes a lot of sense. And it seems so empowering."

Milind nodded. "It is. The more you accept yourself, the more powerful you become. You learn to help yourself, grow your mindset, and take action. Reflection becomes your tool for learning, and you understand that success is mostly about consistency. You realise that not everyone is meant for you, and you find your way and your people."

"And what about money?" I asked.

"Understand it," Milind replied. "Learn to manage and invest it wisely. And always remember, miracles happen when you are true to yourself."

I was thoughtful. "You know, bhaiya, this talk has opened my eyes. I've been so focused on external validation because of my stammer that I forgot to work on myself."

Milind patted me on the back. "It's never too late to start. Accept yourself, work on your mindset, take consistent action, and reflect on your journey. And remember, it's okay to be imperfect. Perfection is a myth. What matters is progress."

"Thanks, bhaiya," I said, genuinely moved. "This has been an eye-opening conversation."

"Anytime, Mehul," Milind replied with a warm smile. "Just remember, the inside-outside approach is key. Build yourself from within, and let that shine through in everything you do. That's the true essence of personal branding."

As we wrapped up our dinner and conversation, I thanked Milind for all the lessons he had imparted and for being such a good host. My train left early the following day, and I was ready for a quick nightcap.

The following morning, I came downstairs to find Milind there with a packed breakfast for me. Surprised, I said, "I'll get some in the train, bhaiya."

"Yes, but not what *Maushi* made. Here's some Misal Pav for you. *Maushi* is determined to feed you. I think she liked you a lot," Milind laughed.

I smiled and thanked him, telling him to thank *Maushi* from my side. I took out a 50 rupee note from my pocket and gave it to Milind to give to her.

"Sure, I will," Milind said as he took the money. "But, what about my fees?"

"Umm... yo.. your fees.." I stammered as I had totally forgotten about it.

"Remember, you asked about my fees over the phone, and I told you I'd ask for it when the time came," Milind reminded me.

"Ye.. yes, bhaiya," I said, embarrassed. "I don't have much money now, but I'll send it to you later."

Milind laughed and said, "No money order can pay my fees. I helped you, not because I know your father or because Amit bhai told me to. I helped you because I heard the determination in your voice despite your nervousness. I knew you were a warrior, and I was right. You will soon become a champion."

I smiled as Milind continued, "When you succeed, remember this moment. No matter your profession or position you're in, I want you to pay it forward."

"Pay what forward?" I asked, confused.

"'Pay It Forward' is a phrase. What I have taught you, teach it to others. Inspire and guide others as I've done for you. That will be my true fee, my *guru dakshina*. Never settle for just one thing. Keep working and keep learning, and you'll achieve things beyond your wildest dreams. Once you achieve success, start helping others who are like you. Don't just live for yourself; live for a greater purpose—a purpose of giving, caring, and contributing to the world that has blessed you with so much. Our time on Earth is brief, so make the most of it for yourself and for others. This purpose will be your source of motivation."

With teary eyes, I hugged Milind and bowed down to touch his feet.

Surprised, Milind said, "It's okay, please don't do that."

"You're my elder, my guru, and my inspiration. If I can be even half of what you are and help others as you've helped me, I'd consider it my success," I said.

With that, I bid him goodbye and headed to the station.

18

"Treat people like people because we are in the same boat; we are in the same storm. Some have yachts, some have canoes, and some are drowning. Just be kind & help when you can."

~ Damian Barr

Life Lessons

Sitting on my train to Baroda, I felt a renewed sense of purpose. Building my inner brand was not just about professional success but becoming a better, more authentic version of myself. With Milind's wisdom guiding me, I was ready to embark on this journey of self-discovery and personal growth. His words resonated with me as I bid him goodbye in the morning.

"Do not ask how I get a job; ask what problem I can solve for any company. Think about this. If you don't know how to solve a problem, learn it. But before that, identify the problem. Never stop learning. The most dangerous thing you can do with yourself is stop learning after traditional education. Keep going. Keep moving. And, remember to pay it forward."

And that, I resolved, was going to be my life mantra.

I took my notebook out and started reading everything I had written in the last three life-altering days, scribbling down my learnings.

1. **Self-Acceptance**: Embrace who you are to become powerful and learnable.
2. **Self-Help**: You must help yourself before you can help others.
3. **Growth Mindset**: Individual growth is tied to mindset growth.
4. **Action Over Inaction**: Not taking action is more dangerous than positive distractions.
5. **Reflection**: Learn through reflection and consistency.
6. **Realistic Success**: Success is mostly about consistency.
7. **Uniqueness**: Understand that not everyone is meant for you, and you are not for everyone.
8. **Financial Literacy**: Understand, manage, and invest money wisely.
9. **Authenticity**: Miracles happen when you are true to yourself.
10. **Brutal Honesty**: Be honest with yourself to make sound decisions.
11. **Discipline Over Talent**: Discipline is more important than talent.
12. **Action Over Intentions**: People judge you by your actions, not your intentions.
13. **Imperfection**: Embrace imperfection as a part of progress.
14. **Core Strength**: Build a strong core personality to adapt to different roles and challenges.

Focusing on these principles can help you build a strong inner brand that reflects your true self, ultimately leading to a more balanced and fulfilling life. Stop comparing yourself with others, be your unique self, and create your own brand.

Epilogue

2018

As the applause from my TEDx Talk faded, I stepped off the stage, my heart still pounding with excitement. The journey from a stammering, introverted child to a confident speaker and trainer has been incredible. Today, as I reflect on my life, I can't help but think back to the first training session I had with Milind, which changed everything for me.

Back in 2005, I was a young man with big dreams but crippling self-doubt. Milind's guidance was a beacon of hope. He taught me the importance of building an authentic inner brand and focusing on personal development. His words, "Everything starts with you," became my mantra.

Soon after our training session, I landed my first job as a Maintenance Engineer, a role I had always aspired to. The confidence Milind instilled in me was evident in my work. My stammering faded away as I grew more self-assured. I became known not just for my technical skills but also for my effective communication and leadership qualities.

Over the years, my career took unexpected turns. My confidence and ability to connect with people led me to a sales job. Initially, I was hesitant, but I embraced the challenge. I discovered that sales were not just about selling products; it was about building relationships and solving problems. I thrived in this environment, breaking sales records and earning accolades.

As I grew in my career, I never forgot the promise I made to Milind—to do more in life. I realised that while my job was fulfilling, I wanted to make a broader impact. Business was in my blood, and I knew that entrepreneurship was the ultimate test of personal development. It was a way to challenge myself and help more people.

So, I made the bold decision to leave my stable job and start my own business. The transition was far from easy. I faced immense challenges, from securing funding to building a team. There were moments of doubt and fear, but I remembered Milind's lessons. I knew that personal victory had to come before the public triumph.

In the early days of my business, I encountered numerous problems. However, despite the challenges, there were many rewarding moments. Seeing satisfied customers, receiving positive feedback, and hitting financial milestones were all testament to our hard work. The most fulfilling aspect was knowing that we were making a difference in people's lives.

Looking back, I realise that the journey of entrepreneurship is a continuous process of growth and learning. It is the ultimate test of personal development. The skills I acquired over the years—resilience, adaptability, leadership, and empathy—were all put to the test.

As I conclude my TEDx talk, I can't help but feel grateful for the path I've taken. It all started with a stammering boy who was determined to overcome his fears. With the guidance of a mentor and a relentless focus on personal development, I transformed my life.

And this is not the end. The journey continues. There are more challenges to face, more goals to achieve, and more people to inspire. I am committed to paying it forward, just as Milind asked me to. I want to help others discover their inner strength and achieve their dreams.

So, if you're with me, let's embark on the next chapter. Let's talk about how to build a winning team that works better than you and how to create a scalable business that stands the test of time.

Are you ready to hear about it?

About the Author

Manish Upadhyay is a Growth Consultant, Peak Performance Expert, and Entrepreneur. His highly interactive and engaging training method is unparalleled. With extensive experience conducting training sessions, he has the ability to make people feel at ease, happy, and comfortable. He is the driving force behind OPEN BOX Consulting, a consulting and training firm he founded. He specializes in Peak Performance Coaching and High-Performance Team Building.

The concept for this book was born from his successful workshop, "Brand in You." Since beginning his training career in 2012, he has trained over 65,000 people individually and through various companies, including Ford, HDFC, SBI Life, and D.Y. Patil University, among many others. He has conducted training not only for people in India but also in the UAE and the US.

In addition to his business endeavors, Manish is actively involved with the Lila Poonawalla Foundation and the Indian Stammering Association as part of his Corporate Social Responsibility (CSR). His connection with the Indian Stammering Association is particularly personal, as he overcame a stuttering challenge.

Empowering Growth: How Manish Upadhyay Transforms Teams and Individuals

In my company, I not only hold a senior position but also happen to be a key connector to the sales department. My job has become easier since I started hiring Manish to conduct various training sessions. He builds their spirit, and the work gets done. My workload has halved, and my team always feels positive, realistic, and on their toes.

Ashwini Shivram
Head HR & CSR
Electronic finance limited

Training comes naturally to Manish. He is made for training and improving the capabilities of those around him. He can empathize and understand the problems and challenges of both business and people. He is sensitive to development needs, and that's what makes him a good trainer.

Saurabh Mulmuley
Deputy Vice President- L&D, OD & TM
Bajaj Allianz Life

The 'Brand In You' Personal Development Program is highly regarded by those looking to invest in their personal and professional growth, with a focus on building a strong and authentic personal brand.

Kevin John James
Management Student
SCMS Cochin School of Business

We decided to hire Manish Upadhyay again because we find his training resources excellent. He revitalizes the team with renewed energy when things start to feel a little stale and flat at work, helping us reinvent ourselves by finding a fresh approach. Thank you once again, Manish.

Late Shri Viren Thakkar
Director
Logistic Park

It was an awesome experience. I am very grateful to you, sir, for such an interactive time management session. Your golden statements are different from those of others, and I truly appreciate them. "The magic of living is giving"—I have experienced this as well. It was a fantastic feeling. Without emotional attachment, goals are just something; with emotional attachment, they become everything. It's the way to become passionate about our aims. You taught me how to honestly say no to people. Being sincere with yourself allows everything to go right, with sufficient time. It was truly a fabulous time with you, sir. I am thankful to you from the bottom of my heart.

Kirti Rahangdale
Scholar- Lila Poonawala Foundation

I have worked with Manish Sir on a few L&D projects for middle management, and it was transformative. The batch he led demonstrated remarkable gains in productivity and performance, earning accolades from both HODs and peers. OPEN BOX's post-training support underscored their strong commitment to positive change. Manish Sir's guidance provided fresh perspectives, empowering the team to create and follow their own growth plans. This led to significant progress, with team members eagerly taking on more responsibilities and sharing their knowledge. Collaborating with Manish Sir was an inspiring experience. His commitment and passion for his work make a big difference. I strongly recommend him for L&D projects.

Deepika Lokhande
Manager, Performance & Training
ZIM Laboratories

I have been working as a real estate professional for the last eight years. I have attended many training programs throughout my career and learned a lot from them. Recently, I completed a training session with Mr. Manish Upadhyay, which has benefited me greatly. I learned the fundamental principles and foundations to achieve success in day-to-day activities. Manish Sir's teaching technique and approach were very simple yet effective. This session has significantly helped me understand how I can achieve my desired goals and shape my future. Highly recommended.

Mithun Waghmare
Leading Real Estate Professional

Hello, I am Swarali Jagtap, a final-year B.Tech E&TC Engineering student at MKSSS's Cummins College, Pune, and a Lila Girl 2018. I want to share what I learned from this workshop. Before that, I must say it was the most impactful and interactive workshop I have ever attended. It was held from the 3rd to the 5th of December.

Sir, you are a great motivational speaker and an experienced trainer. During the session, you covered many important topics, and you gave real-time examples from which we learned and gained a lot of insights. You made the session very interactive and encouraged us to speak up and share our ideas. You also conducted many virtual activities that made us think critically. Truly, you are a hero in your own life, so decent and honest, and you know every small trick. You really made our day, and this was an eye-opening session for me.

Thank you so much, sir, for arranging such a session. I look forward to attending more workshops like this. With lots of respect,

Swarali Jagtap.
Scholar- Lila Poonawala Foundation

Dear Manish Sir, we would like to put it on record that we are highly satisfied with the training workshops you conducted twice for our employees. Your approach was highly effective and made the training very engaging. Thank you for your quick responses and positive attitude each time.Great job!

Sameer Fuley
HR-Head, Logistic Park

Dear Manish Sir, I would like to thank you, as I have never attended such a learning session that was so effective, motivational, and inspirational. I would love to join more of your training programs on different topics.

Thank you,

Aundra Kumar Singh
Leading NBFC Sales Professional

I know a person who is extremely successful, highly experienced, and respected by many in the local business community. He advised me to get help from Manish Upadhyay, and now I understand why he made that recommendation.

Reeta Gupta
HR-Head, Sequel Ford

OPEN BOX Consulting's training workshops are engaging, not at all heavy for the trainees, and are conducted very effectively by Mr. Manish Upadhyay. He sets the right example by being punctual, organized, and straightforward. Yet, there is a certain ease and energy about his workshops that make employees look forward to having the OPEN BOX team in the conference hall! The OPEN BOX team has a great understanding of the problems SMEs face, their pain points, and ways to resolve them. Their approach is both practical and fresh, allowing everyone in the room to relate. People open up easily to him and are willing to see things from a different perspective. The best thing about OPEN BOX training workshops is how well people embrace them. Great job, OPEN BOX!

Jitendra Wasnik
Chairman, NCMCC Society Ltd.

"Excellent mentor and trainer I have ever seen."

Dr. Tushar Somnathe
Director/Head, Centre for Industry Academia Partnerships, Placements & Corporate Connect, Career Development Centre

Mr. Manish Upadhyay is a gem of a person. I am so honored and happy to say that I have never met someone like him in my entire life. Over the years, I have attended multiple sessions from various personality trainers, but I never gained much from them. In fact, I often slept through them, cursing myself for wasting time. However, Mr. Manish's sessions were different. He is the only trainer who became a friend, and after attending his session, I felt it was truly worthwhile and wanted to attend more. This was the first time, and likely the last, that I have gained so much from a personality-enhancing program.

His approach is unique and absolutely wonderful, unlike anything I have seen before. The way he understands people is mind-blowing; his ability to make us feel comfortable and delve deep into ourselves is astonishing. Before you know it, he will have understood you inside out, to the extent that he might even know exactly when you want to talk something out! It is remarkable how he points out things about yourself that you might not have even realized, but which are true.

I am super glad I attended his session and had the chance to interact with him. His positivity, the way he handles people, and his graceful demeanor are qualities I aspire to incorporate into my own life. His approach focuses on the overall development of your personality, attitude, and everything that makes you who you are. His honesty in what he does and his commitment to those he trains make him special and set him apart from others. He has indeed cast a significant influence on me, which I believe will last for a very long time. I strongly recommend Mr. Manish for any kind of personal training, and I am looking forward to more interactions with him.

I wish him the best in all his career and life endeavors. Thank you, Manish! You are awesome!

Deepu Raveendran Unnithan
Management Student, NTPC School of Business
(Mentored by IIM-A)

www.ingramcontent.com/pod-product-compliance
Lightning Source LLC
LaVergne TN
LVHW061547070526
838199LV00077B/6941